EDUCATION FOR INNOVATION

EDUCATION FOR INNOVATION

EDITED WITH AN INTRODUCTION
BY
DANIEL V. DE SIMONE

THE QUEEN'S AWARD
TO INDUSTRY 1966

PERGAMON PRESS

OXFORD · LONDON · EDINBURGH · NEW YORK
TORONTO · SYDNEY · PARIS · BRAUNSCHWEIG

Pergamon Press Ltd., Headington Hill Hall, Oxford
4 & 5 Fitzroy Square, London W.1

Pergamon Press (Scotland) Ltd., 2 & 3 Teviot Place, Edinburgh 1

Pergamon Press Inc., 44–01 21st Street, Long Island City, New York 11101

Pergamon of Canada Ltd., 207 Queen's Quay West, Toronto 1

Pergamon Press (Aust.) Pty. Ltd., 19a Boundary Street, Rushcutters Bay,
N.S.W. 2011, Australia

Pergamon Press S.A.R.L., 24 rue des Écoles, Paris 5^e

Vieweg & Sohn GmbH, Burgplatz 1, Braunschweig

Copyright © 1968
Pergamon Press Inc.

First edition 1968

Library of Congress Catalog Card No. 67–31079

Printed in Great Britain by A. Wheaton & Co., Exeter
08 012795 9

CONTENTS

Preface   vii
Introduction   1

PART 1   THE CONDITIONS

1. Creative Engineering and the Needs of Society,
   J. HERBERT HOLLOMON   23
2. Education for Creativity, C. STARK DRAPER   31
3. Engineering and the Many Cultures, JOHN C. STEDMAN   38

PART 2   THE CONCEPTS

4. Factors Influencing Creativity, CALVIN W. TAYLOR   49
       Discussion   61
5. New Directions in Engineering Education,
   WILLIAM BOLLAY   63
       Discussion   73
6. The Process of Invention, JACOB RABINOW   74
       Discussion   92
7. Innovation and Entrepreneurship, RICHARD S. MORSE   95
       Discussion   102
8. Trade-offs and Constraints, ROBERT C. DEAN, JR.   107

PART 3   THE OPPORTUNITIES

9. Educational Objectives in the Preparation of Engineers,
   B. RICHARD TEARE, JR.   117
10. The Motivation and Development of Faculty,
    ROBERT B. BANKS   123
11. Strategies and Teaching Methods, RAY E. BOLZ and
    ROBERT C. DEAN, JR.   128
        Discussion   138
12. Educating Prospective Inventors, JACOB RABINOW   139
        Discussion   144

CONTENTS

13. Preparing Innovators and Entrepreneurs,
    RICHARD S. MORSE ... 147
       Discussion ... 150
14. Improving the Environment for Creativity,
    CALVIN W. TAYLOR ... 154

Concluding Discussion ... 164

Appendix ... 170

Index ... 173

PREFACE

THE preparation of this book began a year ago when it was decided that the ideas which had been developed and exchanged in a conference held at Woods Hole, Cape Cod, should be made available to industry, the universities, government, and the public at large.

The conference was sponsored by the National Academy of Engineering, the National Science Foundation, and the U.S. Department of Commerce. Its aim was to examine the creative processes of invention and innovation, the opportunities for encouraging creative activities in the engineering schools, and the possibilities for developing and supporting creative engineering education.

This was not just another conference—a "folk ceremonial", as Eric Larrabee once characterized such gatherings. There were no yawning participants. It was the first national conference on creative engineering education and, again quoting Larrabee, a way "of finding out which ideas are fresh and nutritive and which have become a little moldy."*

Hence this book, which attempts to organize the informal talks and discussions of the distinguished educators, executives, inventors, innovators, and entrepreneurs who contributed to the Woods Hole meeting.† Their common purpose was to exchange ideas and proposals regarding:

—The influence of the educational environment on creativity: the climate for creativity in the engineering schools; the impact of traditional methods; opportunities for improvement.

—The stimulation of creative engineering education: the teacher and the techniques; in particular, accomplishments, incentives and disincentives.

—The process of invention and how to teach it: the techniques of invention; reducing the obstacles; triggering dormant creativeness.

* L. B. Holland (ed.), *Who Designs America,* p. 324, Doubleday: New York, 1966.
† The Conference members are listed in the Appendix.

vii

PREFACE

—The process of innovation and how to teach it : bringing new concepts to reality; the direction and management of change; the key role of entrepreneurship; design and development; the marshaling of capital and other resources necessary for the innovative process.

—What might be done to support the development of creative engineering education : the economic and sociological realities; the benefits and obligations; the need for cooperation; the practical problems of enlisting support.

Seldom have as many creative individuals been held together, so long, for a common purpose. The delicacy of such an arrangement was once described, with characteristic incisiveness, by Philip A. Abelson. The trouble, he said, is that "men who have the capacity to create have their share of pride and egotism". Bringing them together for joint enterprises, then, requires that they "become so desirous of achieving common goals that they suppress their natural egotism". It also requires extraordinary skill on the part of some guiding hand.

The man who presided over the Woods Hole Conference, guiding the joint enterprise and holding all the creative individuals who comprised it to a common goal, without suppressing their imagination, was Dr. Emanuel R. Piore.

The Conference was interdisciplinary and intersectoral. That is, it included engineers, scientists, humanists, and social and political scientists, who represented the academic, industrial, governmental, philanthropic, and professional sectors of our society. It was not a parochial affair; education is a multi-faceted, national concern.

The attendance had to be limited. Consequently, those who attended constituted a kind of task force for all those who have an interest in education for innovation. This volume brings the work of the "task force" to you.

This book contains fourteen chapters, based upon the major presentations, mostly extemporaneous, which were made at Woods Hole. Although all of the presentations have been substantially edited, none of the resulting chapters materially alters the substance and intent of the original talks.

The presentations were interlaced with discussions, which had to be extensively rewritten and rearranged. It was my purpose to eliminate repetitive or extraneous comments, while preserving the integrity of the dialogue; the reader will have to judge for himself the extent to which these often conflicting goals have been satisfactorily attained. In any case, whatever merit this volume has is due to those who contributed to the deliberations at Woods Hole and whose thoughts, commitments and passions are recorded in the following pages.

In a cooperative undertaking such as this, there are many individuals to whom special acknowledgment is due because of their special contributions. I am particularly grateful to Dr. J. Herbert Hollomon for his encouragement, counsel, and provocative insights; Dr. C. Stark Draper and my other colleagues on the National Inventors Council for the seminal work that provided the basis for the deliberations at Woods Hole; the members of the Technical Advisory Board of the U.S. Department of Commerce for their advice and assistance; the National Science Foundation for its financial support of the Conference; the National Academy of Sciences and the Woods Hole Oceanographic Institution for their gracious hospitality throughout the four days we spent at Woods Hole; and the members and staff of the National Academy of Engineering for their encouragement of this book.

In a more personal vein, I should like to express my gratitude for the assistance of Mrs. Lesley Moore, my secretary, who faithfully typed through draft after draft of what must have seemed a hopelessly deficient manuscript. And finally, a word of appreciation for my wife, who never once complained about all the spouseless evenings and week-ends.

Washington, D.C. DANIEL V. DE SIMONE
July 1967

INTRODUCTION

So far as the mere imparting of information is concerned, no university has had any justification for existence since the popularization of printing in the fifteenth century.

—Alfred North Whitehead[1]

An engineering school that merely imparts information is an expensive waste. Education needs to be kept alive and relevant: as alive as the intensive civilization in which we live, and as relevant as the concerns that linger after reading the morning newspaper. The problem of keeping engineering education alive and relevant is the subject of this book.

Engineering education should encourage students to strive for the mastery of fundamentals, the discovery of the relatedness of things, and the cultivation of excellence. But all the while it should also be a creative experience, stimulating the imagination of students and helping them to prepare themselves for the unresolved contests and the new challenges of an imperfect world. It should encourage them to believe they can do the "impossible" from time to time, even if it means doing violence to precedent. It should ensure, through them, the continued advance and renewal of our society without sacrificing human values.

These are the aims of creative engineering education—that is, *education for innovation*. Taken together, they constitute a formidable set of goals.

NOBLE ILLUSIONS

Engineering is a profession, an art of action and synthesis and not simply a body of knowledge. Its highest calling is to invent and

---

[1] A. N. Whitehead, *The Aims of Education and Other Essays* (Macmillan, 1959), pp. 138–139.

innovate. To shape and nurture the professional attitudes and skills of synthesis and design needed in the practice of this art is therefore difficult in an engineering educational system which, with few exceptions, stresses the acquisition of knowledge and skills of analysis to the virtual exclusion of all else. In the absence of deliberate counter-measures, it is an educational system that stifles creativity.

Consider the typical measure of a student's performance. It is often enough to stamp out whatever inventive and innovative qualities of mind and spirit he may have possessed when he entered school. By and large, his performance is measured by the fidelity with which he feeds back the information he has absorbed from lectures and texts. Perfect feed-back occurs when he gives the right answers to problems that have been assembled for him. These problems are solved through analysis based on unassailable principles of science and engineering.

Creative individuals are oppressed by this regime, and the real world of invention and innovation is foreign to it. Although in school one must never fail, an inventor fails all the time, and is elated in those rare instances when he succeeds. "An inventor" Charles Kettering therefore once remarked, "is simply a fellow who doesn't take his education too seriously." Indeed, Marshall McLuhan has observed that going to school interrupts the education of students, that the outside world is far richer in information than is the schoolroom.

Seldom are students encouraged to see and experience the relevance of their studies to the "outside" world. Yet it will soon be theirs to change, for better or worse. In many respects, Balzac's rich old man characterizes the educational system:

> "So he had grown rich at last and thought to transmit to his only son all the cut-and-dried experience which he himself had purchased at the price of his lost illusions; a noble last illusion of age."

A school fails if it acts simply to transmit the cut and dried.

EFFECTIVE SURPRISE AND THE EXTENSION OF MAN'S CAPABILITIES

We have already used variations of the terms "engineering", "invention", "innovation", and "creativity" and we will encounter them many more times. It would be useful to try to compose some reasonably serviceable ground rules for these expressions or at least

INTRODUCTION

to note the various ways in which they are used by different authors. But we need not abandon our inquiry just because our definitions are imprecise.

No one has ever adequately defined creativity, for example. We all have a feeling about what it means, but we are not quite sure how to define it. It is like trying to define "jazz".[2]

Creativity has become a fashionable term, not because of its legitimate uses, but because of its wanton employment by sloganeers. It is exciting and complimentary to be creative. Thus comes "creative living" if one serves "ABC refreshers" to friends or moves into the "Cubicle Towers". The result is that when serious commentators speak of creativity, the silent response may be due to an overdose of "ABC" or the dullness of the "Cubicle". In this book, we have tried to be legitimate in our use of the word creative.

Creativity threatens change and disruption, which is why creative ideas are less well received than creative appellations. To be creative is to have the quality or power of producing "effective surprise";[3] of causing "to come into being, as something unique that would not naturally evolve or that is not made by ordinary processes".[4] Creativity involves "a response that is novel or at least statistically infrequent, . . . [and] to some extent . . . adaptive to reality".[5] It concerns "something which is new, rather unexpected, and nontrivial".[6] These observations on the meaning of creativity seem adequate for our purposes. We might sum them up and say that creativity involves effective surprise—something novel, unexpected and nontrivial.

What is "engineering"? It is the art of extending man's capabilities. It has been variously described as the "art of the organized forcing of technological change";[7] an unwillingness to accept the

---

[2] It is said that Louis Armstrong, the great jazz musician, was once asked to define jazz. "If I have to tell you that," he is said to have replied, "you'll never know."

[3] Jerome Bruner in "The Conditions of Creativity", H. E. Gruber et al. (eds.), *Contemporary Approaches to Creative Thinking* (The Atherton Press, 1962), p. 3.

[4] *The Random House Dictionary of the English Language.*

[5] Donald W. MacKinnon, "Fostering Creativity in Engineering Students", *Journal of Engineering Education*, Vol. 52, No. 3, Dec. 1961, p. 130.

[6] Myron A. Coler, "The Two Creativities", *Chemical and Engineering News*, Vol. 44, Aug. 15, 1966, p. 73.

[7] Gordon S. Brown, quoting Elting Morison, in "New Horizons in Engineering Education, *Daedalus*, Spring 1962, p. 341.

natural environment and man's status therein as "a fixed and final condition";[8] the art of exploiting and applying the fruits of science and technology for the benefit of mankind; "the art . . . of making practical application of the knowledge of pure science".[9]

Engineering is epitomized in the processes of invention and innovation. As we use these terms, invention is the process of conception. Innovation, which may or may not include invention, is the complex process of introducing ideas into use or practice, and includes the vital element of entrepreneurship. Thus, society benefits from innovation, not from invention alone, and often there is a long lapse between the two. Heron, for example, discovered the principle of the steam turbine engine two millennia before its introduction.

Through invention and innovation, ideas are conceived, nurtured, developed and introduced into the economy as new products and processes; or into an organization to change its way of doing things; or into a society to change its ways of thinking or to provide for its social needs and to adapt itself to the world or the world to itself.[10] This book is about innovation in education for innovation.

THE CONSEQUENCES OF CHANGE

Technological invention and innovation are the business of engineering. They are embodied in technological change. The consequences of technological change are therefore properly a concern of engineering; certainly, they should be studied in the engineering schools.

Technological innovation has been essential to the process by which America has grown and renewed itself. There is a very significant relationship between innovation and economic growth. Although estimates of the contribution of technological progress to increases in the Gross National Product (GNP) are imprecise,

---

[8] Paraphrasing Lewis Mumford in *Technics & Civilization* (Harbinger Book, Harcourt, Brace & World, 1963), p. 52.
[9] *The Random House Dictionary of the English Language.*
[10] See *Technological Innovation: Its Environment and Management* (U.S. Government Printing Office, 1967), p. 2

economists agree that the contribution is substantial.[11] For example, if we compare the change in the labor input (average annual hours of work) with the change in GNP over the period 1947–1965, we note a marked difference between these two factors. The average annual hours of work remained practically constant, while the GNP rose substantially during the period in question. Indeed, the GNP nearly doubled. Without presuming to say how much of this increase in GNP was attributable to technological innovation, in contrast to other factors such as education, it can be said confidently that technological innovation played a major role.

The most dramatic consequence of technological change is evidenced in man himself. Loren Eiseley describes the phenomenon exquisitely in *The Immense Journey*.[12] Recalling the remarkably perceptive observations of Alfred Russel Wallace, Darwin's contemporary and co-discoverer of the principle of natural selection, Eiseley notes that twentieth-century man has precisely the same brain and body as his ancestor of some twenty thousand years ago. The significance of this in the context of our inquiry is that technological innovation, by extending man's capabilities, has obviated the need for *his* evolution and has, instead, changed the world about him. Under the seas and in space, it is *technology* that sustains him, not his outmoded physical attributes.

THE MANIPULATORS

Quite clearly, however, not all of the consequences of technological change are cause for rejoicing. Many of them, such as environmental pollution, are deleterious and avoidable, and call for social and political innovation. But others, such as temporary dislocations of employees, firms and industries, are concomitants of change, which is inherently disruptive—although these, too, require innovative approaches, so that at the very least, they can be anticipated and ameliorated. Still other objections to technology are

---

[11] See, for example, E. Denison, *The Sources of Economic Growth in the United States* (Committee for Economic Development, 1962); J. Kendrick, *Productivity Trends in the United States* (National Bureau of Economic Research, 1961); and R. Solow, "Technical Change and the Aggregate Production Function", *Review of Economics and Statistics*, August 1957.

[12] Loren Eiseley, *The Immense Journey* (Vintage Books, Random House, 1957), p. 89.

spiritual and philosophical, as, for instance, this comment by Mahatma Gandhi:

> "Of what elevation to man is a method of broadcasting when you have only drivel to send out? What mark of civilization is it to be able to produce a one hundred and twenty page newspaper in one night, when most of it is either banal or actually vicious and not two columns worth preserving? What contribution to man has aeronautics made which can overbalance its use in his self-destruction? You are children playing with razors."[13]

Gandhi resented the subjugation of India by the West and wanted to sever the ties which had been established through India's adoption of Western technology. He advocated an abandonment of this technology and a return to the unblemished past. But much as the people of India revered him, they were unwilling to follow his lead on this score.[14] They would not endorse a policy of technological regression.

The lesson for engineering students is that it is unlikely that any society will ever deliberately arrest its technological advance. Therefore, it is the obligation of engineering education to be concerned at least as much with the *quality* of technological change as with its quantity.

It is an error, of course, to hold that the disagreeable aspects of our society are due to science and technology. Rather, the fault lies in the manipulators of change—in an attitude of mind that sacrifices human values to other objectives. Engineering students should know this, for they will be the future instruments of technological change. As John W. Gardner has observed:

> "The truth is that workers in the grimmest moments of modern industrialism were no more miserable than, let us say, the Egyptian slaves who built the pyramids. It is not advanced technology that causes the trouble. The root of the difficulty is an attitude of mind that has never really died out in the world, nor perhaps even diminished greatly since the days of the Pharaohs—a willingness to sacrifice human values to other objectives.
>
> "Modern technology *need not* destroy aesthetic, spiritual and social values, but it will most certainly do so unless the individuals who manage our technology are firmly committed to the preservation of such values."[15]

---

[13] Upton Close, *The Revolt of Asia* (G. P. Putnam's Sons, 1927), p. 232.
[14] Arnold J. Toynbee, *Change and Habit* (Oxford University Press, 1966), pp. 200–201.
[15] John W. Gardner, *Self-Renewal* (Harper & Row, 1963), p. 57.

NOT BY SCIENCE ALONE

Society has properly extolled the achievements and potential of science, which aims at the extension of man's *knowledge*. In the process, however, quite improperly and unnecessarily, we have underplayed the role of engineering and have paid relatively little attention to it in, of all fields, *engineering* education. And this is truly unfortunate for, as we have already noted, engineering is the extension of man's *capabilities*—no less noble an object than the extension of his knowledge. We need first-rate scientists; we also need first-rate engineers.

In the discussions at Woods Hole, it was noted that very few Ph.D. theses in engineering have anything at all to do with creative engineering design, and that creative design courses are available at only a handful of the nation's engineering schools. The great majority of these theses involve abstract, analytic, science-oriented dissertations. Again, to cite this fact is not to detract from the importance of science. Rather, it is to voice legitimate concern over the philosophy and direction of engineering education; for it is quite acceptable for Ph.D. candidates in the *sciences* to profess no interest in the application of new knowledge to the solution of practical problems, but quite disconcerting when most Ph.D. candidates in *engineering* display similar attitudes in their graduate efforts. If engineers, like scientists, are educated in an environment that voices disdain for the practical application of science, then to whom will society turn for the solution of its problems?

THE NEEDS OF SOCIETY

The first and most important aspect of an engineer's education, J. Herbert Hollomon observes in his essay, is to become aware of the character and needs of the society in which he will live. For we cannot intelligently determine the requirements of engineering unless the needs of society are first perceived. Hollomon notes the increasing concentration of human beings in complex metropolitan environments which, by the turn of this century, will more than double in population. In the process we are becoming more interdependent and, in the not-too-distant future, will likely become what Hollomon calls a "non-work" society, faced with social dilemmas of leisure and affluence. In large part, because of technological prowess, we have become the preponderant world power, with all the profound consequences and obligations that stem from this ascendancy. Gradually, we are passing out of the state of being an industrial civilization and becoming a society whose social, economic, and political life is shaped not so much by the industrial mechanism as by the technologies of communication and information processing.[16] We are at the center of an electrically contracted "global village".[17]

We are a society which cannot much longer condone the outrages we commit against ourselves. We have but a little way to go, as history is measured, before the wanton destruction of our environment reaches disastrous proportions. Most of our rivers are cesspools. Flying high over many of our large cities, one sees them straddled by an overhanging sewer of noxious fumes and contaminants. And, as just one illustration of what we do to the land, the ravagement of strip-mining is not truly believable until one happens upon the destitute remains and imagines himself on the moon's surface.

There are other urgencies. We can no longer ignore the tens of thousands of fellow human beings who are slaughtered and maimed on our highways every year. The scales of opportunity must be balanced for those to whom an equal chance at life's chances has been denied. We must do everything that our collective wisdom allows to make peace with nature and with ourselves, and to promote social and economic progress.

These are some of the problems to which Hollomon refers. Of course, they are not solely engineering problems; indeed, the crucial decisions to be made with respect to them are not engineering decisions at all : they are political. But the role of engineering in the solution of these problems is very important, and it is an awareness of this role and a challenge to do something about it that Hollomon urges be made a part of the education of an engineer. This is the kind of ingredient that can make engineering education alive and relevant.

---

[16] Professor Zbigniew Brzezinski described this change, along with others fundamentally affecting the nature of our international relations, in an address to the National Foreign Policy Conference for Editors and Broadcasters at the State Department, June 1967.

[17] See Marshall McLuhan, *Understanding Media: the Extensions of Man* (McGraw-Hill, 1964).

WHERE IS THE TIME TO COME FROM?

In his essay, Charles Stark Draper tells us of some of his impressions of the nature of creative engineering. He sees creative enterprise as the capability of generating novel and effective means to achieve an important, socially relevant end. Among the characteristics of a creative engineer, he lists the ability to recognize key problems, bring relevant knowledge to bear upon them, conceive effective solutions, and carry these through the innovative process. Engineering education should nurture these traits, but fails in many respects, not the least of which is the way it is structured. Draper sees this structure as an array of fragmented disciplines, whose development into fiefdoms for narrow experts eventually became necessary as knowledge grew over the centuries to prodigious dimensions. But he finds the structure no longer tenable in light of the possibilities afforded by electronic digital computers. They are freeing us from the boundaries of these formal disciplines, breaking them down and permitting us to cut across them with facility. Computers promise to be the most profound educational tool ever devised by man.[18]

Masses of data, which till now necessarily consumed so much of an engineering student's time, can be handled by computers. Indeed, data which were previously beyond hope of handling can now be easily processed. The consequences of theories and assumptions can be tested in minutes.

The computer thus *offers* us a new freedom which is of enormous importance to education: it can release the student from the drudgery of computation and give him greater opportunity to utilize his creative powers along lines of excellence. That is a large part of the answer to the question understandably asked whenever changes of substance and technique are proposed in the educational process: "Where in the curriculum is the time to come from to put these new ideas into effect?" Computers can give us time, if we will accept the offer.[19]

[18] See *Computers in Higher Education* (Government Printing Office, 1967), a report of the President's Science Advisory Committee by its Panel on Computers in Higher Education, John R. Pierce (Chairman).

[19] As to the over-all problem of the time required to accomplish educational objectives, see the *Interim Report of the Committee on Goals of Engineering Education*, Eric A. Walker (Chairman) (American Society for Engineering Education, 1967). See, also, the Concluding Discussion of this volume: "The Inelasticity of Time" (Liston and Taylor), "Curriculum 'Cost-Benefit' Analyses" (Draper and Rabinow), and "Variations on a Medieval Theme" (Draper, Taylor, and Bollay).

THE ENEMIES

In the concluding chapter of Part 1, John Stedman continues the inquiry into the compartmentalization of knowledge and describes numerous enemies of creativity.

"We all know who the enemy is," Stedman says. One wonders. They are mostly undercover forces of destruction, disparagement and criticism. Coupled with attitudes of inattention and lack of understanding, they are formidable obstacles to invention and innovation. How do we counteract these obstacles? Stedman says the first thing to do is to pre-condition engineering students: tell them what to expect and how to deal with anti-creative forces.

In a later chapter (Chapter 6), Jacob Rabinow tells us how to work the other end of the problem, which asks, how do societies and institutions cause creative individuals to flower? "Just love them" and what they do, he says. Far from being obvious, Rabinow's observation is profound; it is as "obvious" as the pneumatic tire was after it was invented. What it means to education is that the "loving" of creativity should begin in the classroom.

Stedman catalogues economic and sociological factors that influence invention and innovation within an organization: remuneration, bonuses, prestige, personal satisfaction ("they are using *my* idea"), making resources available (equipment, assistants, time), caution or timidity on the part of supervisors, jealousy on the part of others, innovative phobias on the part of management, opposition on the part of labor. And on a national scale: lack of healthy competition in an industry, misguided patent policies, unsympathetic tax and other laws, bureaucracy and, finally, the dead hand of prestige embodied in the scientific and technological establishment.[20]

Many of these influences are unreasonable and can be discerned by looking closely and very hard at ourselves—and found quite easily, of course, by assessing others. There lurk the "enemies". "The finger points at human nature," Senator Philip Hart has observed; "we should constantly remind ourselves of these less praiseworthy attributes or characteristics and be on our guard against [them]."[21]

Understanding the nature of these human failings should be a part of education for innovation.

---

[20] See Vladimir Dudintsev, *Not By Bread Alone* (E. P. Dutton, 1957).
[21] *Concentration, Invention and Innovation*, U.S. Senate Subcommittee on Antitrust and Monopoly (U.S. Government Printing Office, 1965), p. 1332.

INTRODUCTION

CRITICS RANKED IN ROWS

A number of key observations and proposals are made in Parts 2 and 3. They fall within the compass of six themes, which represent views that were generally shared by all of the authors and discussants who have contributed to this volume. A summary of these themes and their constituent proposals will be attempted here—with some apprehension, for the potential shortcoming of all such condensations is that a continuous, uninterrupted stream of bare proposals can soon become a hortatory bore.

There have been so many criticisms of the educational system that educators must look with dismay upon the seemingly endless orations. They stand in the arena, faced with the immediate tasks of education on the one hand, and an army of critics on the other. Ortega's reflection on this disparate division of labor is revealing:

> Bull-fight critics ranked in rows,
> Crowd the enormous plaza full,
> But only one is there who knows,
> And he's the man who fights the bull.

Yet, not all of the volumes of criticism are valueless; many are sincere efforts to help further the aims of engineering education. From the first years of the Republic, most notably in Jefferson's administration, education has been proclaimed a paramount national concern. Rephrasing Clemenceau's memorable dictum on generals and war, then, the burden of education is too important to be borne solely by our educators. At issue is the national investment in the most profoundly important asset of all: our human resources. In any case, the proposals which follow are made constructively and with due respect for those who man the arena, while we observe.

INVENTORS AND INNOVATORS

The first of the six themes commonly shared at Woods Hole has already been introduced: it is that invention and innovation are the essence of creative engineering. They are essential to technological, social and economic progress and, consequently, are vital to the achievement of domestic and international goals. The development of the *inventive* and *innovative* potential of engineering students should therefore be an active concern of government, industry, the universities and, in the broadest sense, society as a whole. This proposition is not novel and is perhaps obvious to all who are concerned about engineering education. But it is not so evident to the public[22] and it is simple enough to be easily lost sight of, as it appears to have been, for instance, following the orbiting of the first man-made satellite of the earth by the Soviet Union. Although this was a spectacular feat of engineering innovation, which caused tremors in American educational circles, strangely enough it was hailed in this country as a "scientific" miracle, and the educational reforms thereby generated in American engineering schools were *science*-oriented —which brings us to the next theme.

ORPHANS AND DREARY DISSERTATIONS

The second theme is that the art of creative engineering has been orphaned in the engineering schools. There are exceptions, of course, but we are concerned here with the educational system in general. In the years since the Second World War, there has developed in the engineering educational system—not only in the undergraduate, but in the graduate schools—a regrettable and unnecessary schism between the realms of science and engineering. Paradoxically, in the schools of engineering, the art of engineering has been largely neglected. The stress has been on analysis rather than synthesis, on the abstract rather than the messy alternatives of the real world. As we have noted, the subjects typically chosen as graduate engineering theses generally have little to do with the use of technology to solve real social and industrial problems. One looks almost in vain for Ph.D. engineering theses dealing with such problems as environmental pollution and urban transportation—or, much less, the fulfillment of an industrial need. One finds, instead, "dreary dissertations" (Professor William Arrowsmith's description) isolated from contemporary realities. In the *engineering* schools why should not the art of engineering be given at least equal status with science? If not in the engineering schools, then where?

---

[22] "There is little notion of the creative engineer in the mind of the public, although the image of the creative scientist is widespread . . . [E]ngineers are anonymous." Professor Mary-Frances Blade in M. E. Coler (ed.), *Essays on Creativity in the Sciences* (New York University Press, 1963), pp. 112–113.

INTRODUCTION

Charles Kettering, the first Chairman of the National Inventors Council, once noted at a meeting of the Council that the pneumatic tire is one of the greatest inventions, yet goes unmentioned in the textbooks used in engineering schools. "Why?", he was asked. "Because there are no formulas for it," he replied. "Formulas are plentiful for low-pressure steam boilers, however; consequently, engineering students have to study these, even though they are no longer used."

It is true that engineering increasingly requires a sophisticated scientific base, which must be provided; but an engineer is supposed to be more than a mobile repository of knowledge who is adept at attacking single-answer problems. Moreover, as the Woods Hole participants emphasized, science can be taught creatively, too. "Where, anywhere in life," Edwin Land once asked, "is a person given this curious sequence of prepared talks and prepared questions, to which the answers are already known?"

What engineering is supposed to be about is too often ignored in the educational system. Engineering students should come to understand and appreciate that their profession is the art of extending man's capabilities. Graduate students, especially, should be instilled with this sense of mission—and at the same time, with a sense of professional pride in the contributions of engineering to the progress of mankind. The task might be easier if graduate engineering students were encouraged to undertake, in their thesis work, the solution of engineering problems that require creative design.

There were many at Woods Hole who felt that administrative changes might also facilitate a "return" of graduate engineering students to engineering. They proposed that the control of graduate engineering theses be placed in the engineering schools and not in the graduate schools of arts and sciences, whose mission and calling are different from, though relevant to, those of the engineering fraternity.

But most important, a student learning engineering should be permitted to behave like an engineer.[23]

---

[23] See Bruner, *The Process of Education* (Harvard University Press, 1960), p. 14: "intellectual activity anywhere is the same, whether at the frontier of knowledge or in a third-grade classroom. . . . The schoolboy learning physics *is* a physicist, and it is easier for him to learn physics behaving like a physicist than doing something else."

LEARNING HOW TO SWIM

The third theme says, in essence, that the best way to develop and foster inventive and innovative talents in engineering students is to involve them in projects and experiences that stimulate and require such talents. As Dr. Draper put it: "I don't know how you can find out if a guy can swim unless you throw him in the water." At Woods Hole there was general agreement that the creative requisites of invention and innovation, including entrepreneurship, can be developed and that an environment which evokes and encourages inventive and innovative talents can be provided in the educational system.

There are numerous critical skills and areas of knowledge concerning the processes of invention and innovation which can be taught to engineering students—or, through demonstration, at least brought meaningfully to their attention. Among these skills and areas of knowledge are

—The entrepreneurship of new technologically based enterprises.
—The acquisition of venture capital.
—The relationships between large and small firms.
—The "selling" of ideas.
—The appraisal of inventions and technological opportunities.
—The analysis of markets.
—The management of the innovative process in a corporation.
—The role of competition in the advance of technology.
—The influence of such Federal policies as the tax, antitrust, patent, and regulatory laws.
—The allocation and effects of Federal funds for research and development.
—The protection of know-how, trade secrets and inventions.
—The long-term planning of corporate goals.

New approaches and interdisciplinary arrangements among the schools of engineering, law, business, and the social sciences—with important inputs from industry and government—are clearly necessary for the teaching of skills and subjects such as those described above. Qualified individuals, experienced in the intricacies of invention and innovation, could be brought into the academic environment, both as full-time faculty and as consultants. They could help broaden the scope of teaching, contribute to the skills of the faculty,

INTRODUCTION

and enlarge the student's acquaintance with the real-world facets of the engineering and entrepreneurial arts.

The following are examples of the ways in which engineering students could be given an opportunity to become involved in projects and experiences that develop and foster inventive and innovative talents:

—In the teaching of entrepreneurship, the faculty should collaborate with industry and the community to provide opportunities for students to become involved or associated with the initiation of new technological ventures.

—An analogue of the medical internship and the legal clerkship should be considered for engineering education.

—Consideration should also be given to adopting some of the techniques used to train architects—most particularly, those techniques involving the design and critical evaluation of structures, coupled with appropriate rewards for creative accomplishments.

—Civilian agencies of the Federal Government should support design case programs for use in engineering education. The "cases" would be based on unsolved public sector problems.[24]

—A specified number of the nation's outstanding inventors should be honored as such annually and, through appropriate additional inducements, brought to the universities as "masters" to work with students on special design projects.

—Case materials covering the history of major past innovations (the electronic computer and xerography are examples) should be prepared and disseminated by a suitable agency, such as the Commission on Engineering Education or the American Society for Engineering Education. These should then be made available to the universities for supplemental use in such courses as physics and chemistry.

---

[24] The prototype of such a program is being developed by the Office of Invention & Innovation in the National Bureau of Standards. Systems engineering projects, based on public sector problems, will be devised and possibly used in competitions among the engineering schools. Examples of public sector problems: making highways safer, the environment cleaner, cities more accessible, crime riskier. The program will be organized in cooperation with Federal and State agencies having cognizance over these problems. The aims of the program are to acquaint both students and faculty with demanding areas of public need, invite participation in their solution and, most importantly, cultivate the creative capabilities of coming generations of potential inventors and innovators.

—Traveling fellowships for teachers who have distinguished themselves in the teaching of invention and innovation should be established to enable them to demonstrate and introduce their techniques at universities throughout the country.

—Specialists in the use of creative problem-solving techniques should be retained by the engineering schools to give courses to teachers and selected students on the use of these techniques.

—At least one faculty member per campus should be free to devote a substantial part of his academic year to the organization and introduction of teaching programs designed to stimulate creativity.

—Design laboratories should be established in the engineering schools to enable students to work on personally selected engineering problems, thereby gaining experience in the planning, design, development, testing and evaluation of a new product or process.

—A mechanism should be established to bring promising student inventions to the attention of potential users. Students would thus be given an opportunity to try to do something with their conceptions, and would learn that invention is merely a part of the innovative process.

UNDERSTANDING TECHNOLOGICAL CHANGE

The fourth theme concerns the need for greater understanding of the processes of technological change. Although the United States annually commits enormous resources to these processes, there is much that needs to be learned about their nature, consequences and determinants. We know little, for instance, about the influence of tax, antitrust and other Federal policies on technological ventures.

Moreover, existing knowledge about the world of technological change is not only rudimentary, it is disordered. It is compartmentalized in the technical, economic, sociological, legal, and other literature. It needs to be synthesized in a comprehensive, multidisciplinary program, so that key gaps in existing knowledge can be identified and research undertaken with respect to them. Models more representative of the inventive and innovative processes should be devised, ranging from simple descriptive representations to computer and game simulations. Because this program of research would be of value to numerous communities of interest, it should be undertaken by the government in cooperation with the universities, industry, and the professions. Suitable steps should be taken, through seminars, publications, and consultation, to assure maximum communication and exchange of the knowledge and insights developed under the program.

IMPROVING THE EDUCATIONAL CLIMATE

The fifth theme recurs frequently. It is a recognition that the climate for creative engineering education will have to be improved if any of the suggested programs are to be successfully undertaken. It is not enough for academic administrators simply to approve of creativity in education. There must be a favorable environment for both students and teachers. Merely to proclaim the virtues of creativity is familiar tokenism. A favorable environment requires positive support and sympathetic accommodation for innovative faculty members.

The environment for the student is equally important. In most engineering schools, grading practices do not encourage novel departures from, or challenges to, what has been absorbed in class and through study. Feed-back is expected—the closer the student adheres to what is "correct" or accepted, the better the grades. And the better the grades, the more prodigious and passionate the courtship of recruiters at school's end. In short, the grading systems customarily employed in engineering education tend primarily to measure retentive prowess rather than creativity.

Grades are a critical determinant of a student's attitudes and propensities. Creativity, like invention and innovation, is risky. If the system discourages it, why gamble? After years of conditioning, a student may well ask himself: "Who wants creativity?"

The system of grading, as it is commonly practiced in the engineering schools, needs to be evaluated and its positive and negative effects assessed. One recent development, which appears to be gaining favor in many schools, is the option to take at least one course annually on a "pass–fail" basis. This scheme tends to reduce the *riskiness* of being creative. Even in courses where a "pass–fail" system would be inappropriate or too frighteningly new, the creative performance of a student should be taken into account. For instance, the constructive challenge of presuppositions and orthodoxy, the continual search for better ways of doing things, the observation of the familiar in new lights, and the ability to suggest alternative solutions and not just one "right" answer—these are indications of a talent for healthy dissent and creative initiative. Indeed, teachers should strive to identify and encourage traits of originality and inventiveness at all levels of engineering education. If awards and other forms of recognition were given to outstandingly creative students and, particularly, those responsible for inventive solutions to problems, these would do much to encourage creativity.

Putting any of these proposals into effect requires a sympathetic and capable faculty. In many institutions this means new policies regarding the selection and recognition of faculty members. Calvin Taylor lists examples of such policies in the concluding chapter. He notes, for instance, that excellence in the teaching of creative engineering should be recognized as one of the important criteria for judging a teacher's performance. (It should be no less favorably regarded than the production of fat volumes of unread discourse, so many of which consist of tedious pedantry and assorted hieroglyphics, but little else.) As to the selection of *new* faculty members, consideration ought to be given to a candidate's past engagement in important engineering projects and to his inventive or innovative contributions. On a national scale, a "Creative Engineering Teacher of the Year" award could be established as a recognition for excellence in teaching. Moreover, a reasonable portion of the annual budget of an engineering school should be made available for the support of creative teaching methods and the overall development of the curriculum to achieve this end. Finally, Taylor and his colleagues suggest that the organizational structure of a school could be modified in appropriate instances to permit the trial and evaluation of new ideas on an ad hoc basis.

EXHORTATION NOT ENOUGH

The sixth and last theme takes note of the need for greater cooperation among the universities, industry, the foundations, the professional associations and government. Their cooperation is essential to the development and support of creative engineering education. They need to identify and communicate problems and opportunties. For instance, in order that the schools may profit from the experiences of other organizations that have experimented with techniques of creative education, a much-improved system of intercommunication should be instituted—preferably through an existing organization, such as the Commission on Engineering Education or the American Society for Engineering Education.

If, as is commonly assumed, industry and government agencies need and want creative engineers, they should so inform the universities. First, however, they should appraise their own needs. Are they really committed to the disruptive process of innovation? Do they really encourage it?

If they really want inventors and innovators, they should support programs and institutions that produce such individuals. The most penetrating influence in the academic world is not exhortation, but tangible support.[25] Tangible, sympathetic support is an essential element of the innovative process—in engineering education, no less than elsewhere. It gives organizations the *"will to think"*, as William Shockley observes in the Concluding Discussion of this book.

SHORT STATEMENTS ABOUT EDUCATION

In sum, we shall concentrate on six principal themes or propositions: (1) Inventors and innovators are the vital elements of technological change, which is the business of creative engineering; (2) the art of creative engineering has been orphaned in the engineering schools; (3) the creative requisites of invention and innovation can be encouraged and an understanding of these processes can be taught; (4) research on the processes of technological change, including a synthesis of existing knowledge, is needed and should be undertaken on a comprehensive, multidisciplinary basis; (5) improving the climate for creative engineering education requires positive inducements to faculty and students; and (6) greater cooperation among the universities, industry, the foundations, professional groups and government is essential to the development and support of creative engineering education.

---

[25] See, for example, J. R. Pierce, "What Are We Doing to Engineering Education?", *Science*, Vol. 149, No. 3682, July 23, 1965, p. 397: "What we are doing to engineering is alienating it from the productive civilian economy. . . . We are doing this inadvertently: through the nature and magnitude of the support given to university engineering research by defense and space agencies."

DANIEL V. DE SIMONE

Perhaps the most appropriate way to conclude this introduction is to paraphrase the Victorian economist, Alfred Marshall: Every short statement about the needs of education is misleading, with the possible exception of this one.

What is proposed in the following chapters is not an abandonment of science or of the need to master the structure of scientific and engineering knowledge. It is not the establishment of a design-oriented monolith to supplant the predominantly science-oriented regime that now exists in most engineering schools. Rather, what is suggested is a recognition of the essential nature and role of engineering, the learning of engineering by behaving like an engineer, and an increased emphasis on the excitement of discovering for oneself. In short, what is proposed is that engineering education be kept alive and relevant—that it truly be education for innovation.

PART I

THE CONDITIONS

CHAPTER I

CREATIVE ENGINEERING AND THE NEEDS OF SOCIETY

J. HERBERT HOLLOMON

THE development of engineering education since World War II has been very great. The rate of growth of doctorates in engineering is greater than that in any other field, whether we consider liberal arts or science or medicine. Furthermore, the great advances of science and technology in this country have established it as the world's leader in scientific research and in science and technology broadly. These would appear to be reassuring developments. But pleasant statistics have a tendency to lull us into complacency. We cannot afford that luxury.

All of our educational systems need improvement, and engineering education is no exception. There are deeply held feelings that engineering education has become too science-based and has become removed to some degree from the creative act that the engineer or inventor has to perform to bring the results of science and technology to the benefit of society. If an engineer is to do that job, the first and most significant thing that must be imparted in his education is an awareness of the character of the society in which he will live and the kinds of needs that his society is liable to have.

Many urgent problems challenge the engineering profession and its educators. They stem, in the main, from the changing nature of our society, our domestic and international responsibilities, and the increasing demand for a better life and greater opportunity, not only for Americans, but for all humanity. Let us explore some of these problems, for we cannot effectively talk about the needs of engineering until we have reflected on the needs of society. I think it appropriate, therefore, to begin by first examining the nature of our society—the kind of society it is and perhaps will be.

THE URBANIZATION OF AMERICA

The most important characteristic of our society, in my view, is that it is becoming increasingly urban. This concentration of population is occurring not only in the United States, but in the world in general. Increasingly, people live in cities or very near to cities. The majority of the people in the United States live in the megalopolitan areas of the Pacific coast, the Atlantic coast and the area centered around Chicago. Some 75 to 80 per cent of the population—and this percentage is growing every year—live in these complex urban environments. These environments are such that the interdependence of the people, one on another, and on their social institutions, becomes increasingly important. The dependence of the farmer on other people is not nearly as great as the dependence of the urban citizen on the social structure of his city.

A small village does not have serious police problems—in part, I suspect, because everyone in the village knows or knows of everyone else in the village. In a large complex society, however, man becomes essentially anonymous. He becomes a statistic and disappears.

Furthermore, the interaction of man with his environment in the city becomes increasingly complex and provocative. The city produces pollutants which foul the air he breathes and the streams from which he drinks. Yet with respect to these dangers, he is unorganized. Many are the social protests, but not with respect to foul air and water.

Increasingly, therefore, America becomes more urbanized, its people more interdependent, and their environment more hostile and menacing.

THE RISE OF THE SERVICE INDUSTRIES

A second characteristic of our society, which is a corollary of the first, is that we have ceased to be a society tied to the land. A very insignificant number of our people produce the food and fiber which are necessary for the rest of us. I am talking now about agriculture, not food or fiber processing. Only about $6\frac{1}{2}$ per cent of our working population are engaged in agriculture today. This fraction has been decreasing since 1880 and will continue to decrease in the years ahead. Ten or fifteen years from now less than 3 per cent of the working population will be engaged in the agricultural sector of the economy. That is a figure with which I am sure you are all familiar, but now let me go to the next consideration.

Many of us have considered ourselves a manufacturing economy. That also is changing. Less than half of the total working population in the United States are engaged in manufacturing and agriculture together. More than half are engaged in what are termed the service industries. These are the industries that are concerned with the social problems of the city, with recreation, with education, with medicine, with travel, with culture, with the arts, with insurance and all those things in which people who are affluent—people whose basic survival needs have been met—are now engaged.

In the period 1950 to 1960 there were no net jobs added to the manufacturing component of our economy. In other words, there were no increases in the number of workers, either white collar or blue collar, in the manufacturing sector of the economy. That was not true from 1960 to 1965, during which some net manufacturing jobs were added, but this increase is a minor perturbation in the total picture.

Thus, the majority of the workers of our society are engaged in the performance of services which are not a part of the agricultural or industrial sectors of our economy. The services they perform are not required to produce goods or crops or to extract minerals. What this means is that, increasingly, technological challenges will be coming from the "services" sector. We are getting a new mix of clients.

THE ADVENT OF THE "NON-WORK" SOCIETY

A third characteristic of our society, which is related to the first two, is that we are becoming a "non-work" society. Now, I do not know any way to put this other than "non-work". If we add up the total work done per person in the United States per year, comparing the years 1900 and 1960, we find that the amount of work that is done per person per year has decreased by a factor of two. And if we look at the trend over this century, we find that the rate of decrease is increasing, so that in two or two-and-a-half decades we will do less than half the work again, per person, per year that we are doing today.

Let me explain that in a little bit more detail. I am not referring only to the number of hours worked per week. I am also referring to the fact that, increasingly, young people enter the labor force at a later time during their lifetime, and also leave the labor force at an earlier time. The number of weeks of vacation and the number of days of holidays are increasing. In 1985, the average citizen of the United States will enter the work force when he is twenty-five. He will work the equivalent of a forty-hour week for six to eight months of the year and will leave the work force when he is fifty.

The situation will be that we will have become a "non-work" society—I don't know what else to call it—and the reason I call it a "non-work" society is that a larger fraction of one's normal lifetime will be spent not working than working. That is a situation which no non-slave, egalitarian society has ever faced in the history of mankind.

Let's consider what some of the consequences of this change will be. Man's non-work time will give him more opportunity to pursue cultural and recreational activities—and to stare at his television set. The education of people, particularly young people, will have to do less with their ability to create wealth than with their ability to use wealth which has already been created. This will be a profound change in emphasis and will have an impact at all levels of education.

In the election of 1976, the number of "non-worker" voters and worker voters will be about the same. There will be more retired people, more young people, and more other "non-workers", who are not engaged in financially-compensated activities.

I think it important to recognize that as technological innovation increases productivity, we have to decide not only how to dispose of the increased productive capacity, but also how we will use the decreased work time.

We have been living with this problem as long as we have had technological change. Roughly speaking, since 1890 we have disposed of our increased productivity in two ways : we have increased the output of goods and services by approximately 3 per cent per year since 1890, and we have decreased the amount of work that each individual does in the society by about 1 per cent per year. Our real increase in productivity over that period has therefore been 4 per cent per year—and we have been taking a part of it in increased goods and services and a part of it in decreased work.

At any given time that choice, which is political in nature, could be changed. We may wish to take more of the increased productivity either in decreased work or in increased outputs of goods and services.

INTERNATIONAL RESPONSIBILITIES

A fourth characteristic of our society is that we have become increasingly involved in international affairs. We find ourselves responsible for the political stability of much of the world—for example, in Latin America, Asia, and Africa—and we take as a matter of course our involvement in these affairs, although they would have been taken quite differently in the 1930's. In a matter of only three decades, America's views of its international responsibilities have changed remarkably.

This change poses many problems—political, social, economic. It also poses technological problems, for it has to do with the maintenance of a large defense establishment, which depends for superiority on research and development. It has to do with the conquest of space, and I need not elaborate on the importance of science and technology to his vehicle for the maintenance of international prestige. And it has to do with technical assistance in our foreign aid programs.

Engineering education must therefore comprehend these problems, for engineers—no less than economists, lawyers and sociologists—must deal with them.

THE INCREASING INVESTMENT IN TECHNOLOGICAL CHANGE

A fifth characteristic of our society—and it has already reflected itself in engineering education—is that we are investing an increasing fraction of our national resources in science and in research and development. We have become more and more aware of the importance of science and its application to the national defense, the rise of productivity, the production of new products, and the introduction of new processes. This is certainly true in the defense and space establishments and in sophisticated industries such as those in the electronics, chemical and data processing fields.

The increasing allocation of our resources to technological change, the urbanization of America, the decline of agriculture and manufacturing, the rise of the service industries, the advent of the "non-work" society, and the new internationalism—these, I think, are among the primary characteristics of the society in which we live. I should like to elaborate further on some of the social problems these characteristics pose and what they mean to engineering and to engineering education.

CREATIVE APPROACHES TO LARGE SOCIAL PROBLEMS

The social needs of our time become ever larger and more complex and are such that they are not met by the normal functioning of the market place. The reasons are more or less obvious. They are important in the present administration's concern with such matters as air pollution, water pollution, city planning, the horrible problems of the slum, the problems that are associated with adequate water supplies for the future.

Perhaps as important as any of the social problems I have mentioned are the unmet problems of traffic safety. With automobiles, we Americans manage every year to kill 50,000 people, maim 2,000,000 more, and cause destructive property damage of from $8 to $13 billion. Now, the responsibility for doing something about this hideous toll rests with society as a whole, because the free market economy is apparently either unwilling or unable to meet it. If we treated our soldiers in Viet Nam with the same disregard, the mothers of America would rise up and prevent their sons from going there.

Air and water pollution, urban slums, the techniques of traffic safety, the design of vehicles—these are the kinds of crucial social problems which will have to be faced in the near future. And they will have to be met by bold new departures in which creative engineering plays a vital role.

WE ARE NOT SCIENCE-LIMITED

Most of these social problems are not science-limited, and by "science" I mean an understanding of the physical world as distinguished from the social world. There is not much more we have to know about science in order to be able to deal with these problems. The limitations are social, political and economic, rather than scientific. What is needed is, first, the will to solve them and the mechanisms to get at them.

Second, we need to bring together creative persons who, on the one hand, are able to understand the needs of the society in which they live, and, on the other, are sufficiently familiar with the techniques and capabilities of science to be able to invent solutions to the problems which are politically and socially feasible.

Third, we need a new kind of entrepreneurship to bring these inventive, and socially and politically feasible, ideas to fruition. Changing a society is always difficult and the fellow who does that changing is what we call an entrepreneur, an innovator—a person who is willing to take personal risk with respect to the changes he wishes to bring about and to stand behind the revolutionary character of these changes.

I am convinced that entrepreneurship can be taught, that the subject of innovation and how change takes place and is brought about can be taught, and that these subjects should be essential elements of the education of engineers as well as other people engaged in fulfilling the needs of society.

THE "NEW" ENGINEERING

I should say something about what I perceive the trend in engineering to be. In the future engineering will be largely information-based. This may be obvious to most of you, but it wasn't so obvious to me. When one looks at the development of engineering and the engineering schools in America over the last 100 years, one finds that our engineering schools were started primarily to teach agricultural engineering, because we were then concerned with food and the development of the food supplies of this country.

We next saw the development of the engineering arts of mineral extraction. Then we began to develop the materials and chemical processing arts. Still later, with the development of electrical technology we became concerned with energy. Engineering focused on the production, distribution and use of energy.

What has happened since then? It is strange that there are not many first-rate agricultural engineering schools any longer. There are not many first-rate "minerals" schools either. And even the schools which have been known as electric power institutions are disappearing. The "new" engineering will largely be based on information technology—the handling of huge quantities of information, in effective ways, in a complex society.

Thus, the requirements of engineering will increasingly have to do with problems in which the limitations are political, social and economic; in which the solutions will have to be creative but will involve much science already known; in which the engineering is based largely on information technology; and in which the ultimate task of establishing new institutions that are required to bring the changes society needs must be given to the entrepreneur—the innovator.

THE CHALLENGE TO EDUCATORS

In conclusion, I should like to comment briefly on some of the deficiencies I perceive in engineering education. Much of the graduate engineering in America is research based. By this, I mean that it is science-oriented, in that engineers in graduate education are concerned with learning more, rather than learning how to do more.

Increasingly, engineering educators come from universities alone. Their backgrounds have been in the academic world, without experience either as engineers who design, inventors who invent, or entrepreneurs who establish invention-based businesses.

Engineering education has removed itself from a concern with the social, economic and political problems of our time and has become more concerned with the science that underlies and undergirds the engineering we practice.

Moreover, government agencies that support engineering education at the graduate level support the kinds of scientific and technical projects that need to be undertaken in order to advance our defense and space missions.

I want to close, therefore, by expressing the hope that we will begin to deal more intensively with the problems of how to establish a climate in which at least a few of the extraordinarily creative people can put science to work for the *other* needs of man.

CHAPTER 2

EDUCATION FOR CREATIVITY

C. STARK DRAPER

MY IMPRESSIONS of the nature of creative man and his importance with respect to engineering are based on my own experience. I have collected no statistics. I have had no teams of analysts researching anything. This chapter is simply an exploration of some of the ideas I have developed during some thirty to thirty-five years of dealing with new and different situations and challenges.

Creativity, as I see it, is the human quality of imagination and the capability of bringing new and significant innovations into existence. These innovations may be of many kinds and may take such diverse forms as new ideas, devices, systems, and organizations. Innovations are essential for the progress of any nation or society which aspires to leadership and excellence among the peoples of the earth.

Creativity, which is the basis of innovation, is always rare. It cannot be purchased or ordered into being by any authority, however powerful that authority may be. This means that to maintain prestige and power a country must rely on the creative talents of its citizens. Success depends very much upon the identification and development of enough creativity to provide a favorable position in the balance of capabilities among national rivals. The factors involved in this balance are, in fact, across-the-board, including social conditions, science, technology, business and military power.

The discussion that follows recognizes the importance of all these elements, but it is primarily concerned with technology and the development of engineering creativity.

Science, the pursuit of knowledge for its own sake, and technology, the application of knowledge and available materials and resources toward the satisfaction of the needs of society, have both made great contributions to the United States in its centuries-long climb to pre-eminence among nations. Scientists, leading creative studies of natural principles, and engineers, playing a similar role for technology, have been responsible in large part for the innovation from which our greatness has sprung.

Today, this superiority of the United States is being challenged by countries with tremendous resources who are strongly motivated and vigorously working to tip the balance of power toward themselves. In these endeavours, technology is universally recognized as basic and one of the essential competitive factors. It follows that creativity, the source of technological advance, is of great importance not only for national progress, but perhaps for survival itself.

Creativity, an attribute of the mind, exists because of natural talent, but must be supplemented and nurtured by education if its maximum levels of effectiveness are to be realized.

In addition to this obvious function of education, the processes of education provide a means for identifying and encouraging individuals with potential for creativity so that this promise may be developed to the highest possible level.

Because creativity is an essential factor in the effort to realize national goals, and education is a basic means for discovering and developing creativity, it is apparent that education especially adapted for dealing with this talent is a matter of the greatest importance for the United States.

THE ELEMENTS OF ENGINEERING CREATIVITY

Creativity, as I am discussing it, is the capability for generating novel and effective means to achieve a desirable result in dealing with a situation of importance to society. Numerous factors are involved across the full span of creativity. These qualities, all special human capabilities, are—and I know I am going to get a lot of arguments regarding this list:

1. The ability to recognize important situations.
2. The ability to analyze real world circumstances and convert them into manageable problems.
3. The ability to perceive the relationships between these problems and existing science and technology.

4. The ability to imagine solutions where no answers have existed before or to conceive means to accomplish needed results better than those provided by existing arrangements.
5. The ability to plan practical embodiments of these imagined concepts.
6. The ability, either directly or by management, to realize working arrangements that mechanize these concepts.
7. The ability to demonstrate satisfactory operation.
8. The ability to complete the steps to bring an innovation into the effective service of society.

In practice, very few creative individuals have all the capabilities delineated in this list, but the elements of understanding, imagination and at least the beginning of a reduction to practice must be present before the term "creativity" can appropriately be applied.

Of the various qualities involved in creativity, self-reliance and the habit of independent thought are fundamental. Without them, few significant results can be expected. Ability to observe situations clearly, to take the initiative, and to persevere in pioneering work, even in the face of continued difficulties and discouragement, are also essential.

Many resources are available which offer help through the process from technological creation to profitable innovation, but creativity of a high degree can be expected only from individuals acting alone, or in groups, who have great self-confidence and a habit of imaginative thought. These potential qualities can be identified and are best developed by educational programs which differ from the typical educational techniques employed in high school and college education today.

THE ROLE OF EDUCATION

Education is the process of imparting knowledge, nurturing habits of thought, and developing capabilities for action that supplement and extend natural human capability. The fundamental needs of creativity for self-reliance, initiative, and imagination have already been noted. These are all qualities that can be made more effective by proper education.

However, the primary function of education, as it has developed through the centuries and is practiced today, is to train student minds to receive knowledge and to impart the information from which knowledge may be developed. The centuries that have elapsed since the great days of Greece, when one man could hold leadership of thought in all subjects, have seen the fragmentation of education into many disciplines with generally accepted and often quite impervious boundaries between them. This state of affairs has developed because studies from many standpoints are now required to attack the complex circumstances of the human environment.

From the beginning and through the years, each view of this single world presented problems so difficult and extensive as to require substantially all of the attention available to specially motivated groups of individuals. Thus science, an overall field with many specialities, came into being. Technology, developing from science, naturally followed the same course and became fragmented into many more or less independent areas.

Today, scientific knowledge of the real world has advanced to the degree that utilization of the great repositories of available information by means of mathematical methods or by computers has made feasible moves beyond the artificial boundaries of formal disciplines.

This breaking down of barriers is being forced by man himself, who has become accustomed to conceiving and reducing to practice systems of such complexity that he now deals simultaneously with advanced phases of knowledge, practice, and arrangements that can be effective only if all elements are thoroughly understood and brought into synchronization.

The recently completed Gemini V mission is an example of cross-disciplinary success—education, technology, research and management, brought together a single great system meeting stringent requirements for high performance and reliability in all of its components. Tremendous breadth and depth of knowledge and wisdom have been required of the men who have already created a spectacular system for space exploration—a system that will surely be expanded and provided with much greater capabilities in the near future.

Aerospace developments are not an isolated example. Many other military and civilian systems now in use or under development are multi-disciplinary in their design and operation.

Obviously, high imagination and deep knowledge covering numbers of related fields are essential for success in these endeavours.

EDUCATION FOR CREATIVITY

Education, as it is generally practiced today, from middle high school years through the academic undergraduate and graduate processes in institutions of higher learning, is admittedly effective in building up the formal knowledge of well motivated, hardworking students interested in particular disciplines. However, the same statement cannot be made for the identification and nurturing of the unique qualities of self-reliance, imagination and effective reduction to practice.

NEW APPROACHES ARE NEEDED

There is no doubt that educational methods for the development of these qualities—the very foundations of creativity—can be improved. The matter at issue is the dichotomy in method which will (1) build within the student an organized body of knowledge of a specific field and (2) identify and nurture the qualities of mind that depend to a considerable extent upon inspiration and which are not susceptible to immediate and unambiguous evaluation.

In the first case, formal marks gained under the supervision of teachers dealing with textbook material supply much of the motivation that drives students toward knowledge and self-development. This system works well as far as it goes, but it unfortunately causes students to look for problems set into definite terms, and results in their dependence on instructors for help with solutions. It emphasizes rewards in terms of grades for the degree of success achieved in reaching a predetermined solution, rather than for the novelty of the solution offered.

Failure to produce good results leads to nothing more than lowered marks. This mechanism is effective for imparting knowledge, but it does not particularly encourage imagination or inculcate habits of independent thought and action.

This defect is especially bad because it builds up habits of noncreativity and complete dependence on problems and solutions stated by others. Unfortunately, conditions for the development of this undesirable mental attitude are most favorable during the formative years when initiative and self-reliance should be nurtured to the greatest possible extent.

In effect, the usual course of education provides students with answers to conventional questions, without much attention to situations not yet resolved into definitely stated problems. Whole careers of some distinction are often devoted to searching for questions to fit relatively small variations of the answers learned in school.

Primary attention should be given to the dilemma posed by the necessity of teaching facts and predetermined methods during the prime years when the student is most susceptible to development of mental attitudes favorable to independent and creative thinking. This question is difficult, but not impossible to solve.

In order to acquire a background of and familiarity with available knowledge, formal education is indispensable and must be continued until the student has developed both learning skills and a backlog of basic information in science and the humanities.

If human beings were machines with a storage capability for all factors encountered in any order, knowledge resources could be completed before starting the development of habits and capabilities for applying these resources to creative solutions of complex problems. This is generally no more possible than a football player becoming great by learning only fundamentals, without the maturing experiences of actual play.

Education for creativity, then, as distinguished from learning to acquire knowledge, is characterized by opportunities for students to deal independently and directly with situations requiring creative action. Only by experience acquired in this way can natural talents be developed toward their maximum potential for significant service to society. To be truly effective, experience, imagination and initiative must be balanced by resources and knowledge great enough to prevent wasted effort on already solved problems on the one hand and, on the other hand, missed opportunities due to imperfect information on the facts of science or the existing state of technology.

The need for special attention to the imaginative phases of creativity has been recognized in many places. Corrective steps have been in progress on relatively small scales for some time. Science fairs for high-school students, and special problems and project laboratories for undergraduates are now directed toward developing imagination and capability for independent action during the days of higher academic education.

Laboratories of technology are beginning to provide postgraduates with internship experiences similar to those that have long been available in medicine and law. Details of operation for these laboratories are as yet not generally known or accepted as good practice, but the excellent results, small in number as yet, that have been achieved suggest that educational attention to creativity will surely pay large dividends in benefits for the nation and for our society.

The future holds many interesting possibilities, of which future contributions by creativity are among the most important. Education can and must be expected to provide support for these endeavors.

CHAPTER 3

ENGINEERING AND THE MANY CULTURES

JOHN C. STEDMAN

WE HAVE heard a lot about the ingredients that go into making up the "creative man". We have heard, also, about the foreign elements that the "too many cooks" may throw in to spoil this fine broth. We have centered our attention, in short, on the man himself and the things inside him, both inherited and acquired, that make him more or less creative. I want to explore some of the outside forces and factors he is likely to run into—usually after he has completed his formal education—that may prevent or discourage him from fully using his creative talents.

PSYCHOLOGICAL THREATS TO CREATIVITY

We all know who the enemy is: It is the director of research who puts the creator to work concocting a piece of plexiglas that looks like sandpaper on TV, when he would like to work on a cure for stomach ulcers. It is the sales manager who tells him his new-born idea looks as though it came out of the zoo and no one in his right mind would ever fall in love with it. It is the patent counsel who tells him it is too obvious to be patentable, but at the same time he shouldn't let anyone in on the secret. It is the general counsel who insists that if he goes to work for a competitor he must forget everything he has learned. It is the accountant who points out that he cannot be expected to budget hard dollars for a project without even knowing how much money it will make for the company in 1969.

These are the people I am going to talk about: the people who stand in the way, who block and frustrate, who throw cold water on ideas, and eventually reduce the creative man to an unmotivated, unimaginative, quiescent, discontented routineer.

Let me emphasize that I approach the subject as an unlettered layman. I know nothing about engineering and I know nothing about psychology, or, for that matter, creativity. Let me emphasize, also, that I am not talking about that rarity, the uncommon man. Some creators, I suppose, never lose their way. Their determination, facility and singleness of purpose carry them through, and enable them to triumph over all obstacles. As one recent writer put it: "A man of the stuff of which great inventors are made will invent under any circumstances and conditions."*

If they were all like this, we would have no worries. But they are not. As the writer I just quoted pointed out:

"Industries move forward as much by the efforts of not-so-great inventors and through the creative contributions, large and small, of many earnest people whose cumulative work constantly brings us to new horizons. . . . What really matters is that a climate exists that creative people do benefit from."

People, most people, do need encouragement and motivation. The chilling frosts of obstruction, disparagement, criticism, inattention, and lack of appreciation and understanding, are more than they can take, unless they have been subjected to pre-exposure conditioning. And so, it behooves us to take a look at the nature and sources of these obstructive and destructive factors.

Examination of the outside obstructions to creativity starts with study of the incentives or motivations for creativity. But these need not detain us. The important factors that contribute to the internal development of creativity will be covered in other chapters and those that contribute to the salutary use of that creativity are fairly self-evident. The factors that *obstruct* creativity or its application are not so clear.

It is appropriate to consider first the outside forces and factors that obstruct creativity, that chill and kill imagination, curiosity, determination, originality, enthusiasm, independence and the other ingredients of creativity. These obstructive forces can operate, of course, during the educational process, but they may persist even more tellingly later on. College graduates, after all, do not necessarily develop an immunity to the familiar psychological and

---

* J. A. Haddad in *175th Anniversary of the U.S. Patent System*, Vol. 1, p. 237. Patent Office Society: Washington, D.C., 1966.

cultural barriers: the fear of failure or excessive desire for success; the fear of ridicule and disapproval; the predisposition toward caution, conservatism and conformity; the stultifying forces of discouragement, excessive pessimism, excessive self-criticism, and lack of confidence; timidity and lack of legitimate aggressiveness; lack of persuasion, articulation and sense of legitimate strategy; predisposition toward over-competitiveness or a lone-wolf attitude that results in too much secrecy; the enervating effect of limitations on freedom and experiment, excessive supervision and blue-printing; and so on.

The army of demons is always there, ready to move in, awaiting only the aid and assistance of any who will provide it, accidentally, inadvertently, deliberately or mistakenly. The weapons are varied. We have all encountered the so-called "killer phrases":

"We tried something like that years ago."
"That's ridiculous."
"That's too radical."
"Let's form a committee to consider it."
"That's contrary to policy."
"Has anyone ever tried it?"
"It won't work."
"That's too obvious to be considered."
"That's superficial."
"That's interesting, but we don't have the time—or manpower."
"Tell me right now—what's the potential profit from it?"
"That's not the kind of idea we expect from you."

So much for the psychological forces that threaten the creative nature of the man, as such.

ECONOMIC AND SOCIOLOGICAL THREATS TO CREATIVITY

Let me turn now to another set of factors, largely economic and sociological, whose presence may inspire creativity and whose absence may destroy it. Creative man, even the uninhibited one, needs some motivation other than his innate creativity, not only to get him started but also to keep him going. He is not, typically, a juggernaut and probably not a self-starter.

As I see it, the outside forces that contribute to motivation fall into four categories. I am not listing these in any order of importance. The relative importance may be quite different for X than for Y. First are the economic or monetary factors, such as higher salaries, bonuses, prizes, promotion and the like. Second are contributions to prestige and recognition by one's peers, one's superiors or the public in general. These are reflected in titles, again in promotion, and in public recognition of various kinds: for example, speeches, articles, symposia, one's name in patents. Third is the satisfaction that comes from adoption and use of one's ideas, the more widespread the better. Fourth, there is the general and specific assistance that contributes to all of these: affirmative aids, suggestions, encouragement, guidance, furnishing of equipment and helpers, and so on.

These factors, when present, encourage creativity and the use of creativity—in varying degrees depending upon the circumstances and the make-up of the creator. Their absence discourages creativity and its use. This we recognize. What we may not recognize is the variety and complexity of the circumstances that may prevent these incentives from working the way they should. Sometimes the withholding of the incentive is real. Sometimes it is only apparent. Sometimes it is justified. Sometimes it is not. Sometimes it is understood and accepted. Sometimes it is misunderstood and not accepted.

Let me suggest, merely as illustration and without elaboration—since many of them are spelled out in a report of the National Inventors Council* and will be discussed by Professor Bollay in Chapter 5—some of the circumstances that may legitimately prevent the disclosure, acknowledgement or usage of creative ideas. They include (1) the need for obtaining patent protection; (2) the protection of trade secrets; (3) the hard evaluation of new ideas in terms of profitability; (4) the equally hard balancing of the costs of innovation against the possible returns.

Other considerations may be involved which are less legitimate, at least from the point of view of the creator himself and the public in general, however legitimate they may appear to the corporate decision-makers. The latter may be motivated, for instance; (1) by the lack of substantial need, demand or competitive pressure; (2) by caution, timidity, uncertainty and a disposition to procrastinate; (3) by resistance to change and new ideas; (4) by a psychological opposition to things that others suggest or may get the credit for;

* *Report of The National Inventors Council on Engineering Education* (Washington, 1965).

(5) by a live-and-let-live policy that shies away from disrupting the industry and stirring up one's competitors; or (6) by discouragement or frustration that stems from pervasive opposition to innovation both inside and outside the company.

Or, the decision-makers may be influenced by such factors as labor opposition to labor-saving devices, or opposition from other influential interests that might be injured by the innovation.

Finally, misjudgments may result from sheer incompetency, obtuseness, misinformation as to facts, or just plain arbitrary action. These could include, for instance, crediting the wrong person with a given idea, misjudging the commercial value of a given contribution, or denying recognition on the ground that the creator merely did what he was hired to do. I need not elaborate on these. They are things we can sometimes find by taking a hard look at ourselves, and can find quite easily by taking a hard look at others.

This is not the place to argue whether episodes of the sort I have mentioned—and one could continue to spin them out *ad infinitum*—are resolved wisely or unwisely. The point is that every decision that fails to provide appropriate reward or recognition for an employee's creative idea or prevents its usage carries with it the possibility, though by no means the certainty, of discouragement, frustration, disappointment, resentment, and an ultimate lessening of creative effort. The further point is that in many instances, though by no means all, the unfortunate side effects of such decisions could be eliminated or reduced—sometimes by arriving at a different or modified decision; sometimes by better understanding on the part of the decision-maker of the reaction and the motivations of the creator; sometimes by a better understanding on the part of the creator of the reasons behind the decision. And the final point is that any reduction or elimination in these side effects is likely to mean improved performance by the creator with ultimate benefit to the creator himself, his employer and the public at large.

BRIDGING THE GULF

It is fairly clear, I think, where the educational process fits into this picture. There are bound to be business and administrative decisions that leave the creator unhappy. But certainly we should strive to keep these to the minimum. And the greater the decision-maker's understanding of the creator, what motivates him and how he ticks, and the greater the creator's understanding of what is behind the decision-maker's judgment and how *he* ticks, the greater the probability of wise decisions that are accepted as such.

Professors Bollay and Taylor point out that engineering schools are in a position to develop creative people if they train their students in the creative processes. I suggest that engineering schools, in cooperation with business schools, law schools and other appropriate social science disciplines, can maximize the affirmative contribution of creative people by training both the creators, and those with whom the creators must deal, in the arts of communicating with and understanding each other. This education in mutual understanding might be effectuated in various ways. In our society, after all, technological creativity has become too important to have it lessened or frustrated by a lack of mutual understanding and a failure of communication that, with a little effort and education, could be avoided.

SPILL-OVER AND SIDE EFFECTS

Let me add a few words about this matter of mixing disciplines. The usefulness of cross-disciplinary activity of the type I have been talking about is not necessarily limited to increased understanding and cooperation in the areas under discussion. It may have salutary side effects in at least two other respects.

The first aspect relates to the phenomenon that has been referred to in passing two or three times, namely, the occasions on which prepared, sophisticated, knowledgeable outsiders—outsiders, in other words, who have learned a subject without being inhibited by the grinding sort of education that Professor Taylor will describe in Chapter 4—make unusual, unexpected and really tremendous contributions to a particular art.

Engineers are familiar with cases in which solutions to engineering problems have come from outside their profession. The same thing happens in practically every discipline. Some of our more thoughtful writers have addressed themselves to this phenomenon. The recent massive work entitled *The Act of Creation*, by Koestler, for instance, talks about "bisociation" as distinguished from "association", and discusses in that connection the practice of shifting gears, so to speak, and applying what one has learned in one field to an entirely different field.

I suggest that this phenomenon could be expected to occur and work usefully in the cross-disciplinary process I have been talking about. Just as the engineers, in given circumstances, can make a genuine contribution to the law, or to psychology, so the psychologist or the lawyer may be able to make a genuine contribution to engineering once he knows enough about the subject. The cross-disciplinary approach should be one of the most effective ways of acquiring this knowledge and directing it into innovative channels.

The second aspect relates to creativity in the social sciences. Creativity exists in technological fields; it also exists in the humanities: in the arts and music, literature, and so on.

The social sciences, and I am defining them broadly for present purposes, seem to me quite backward in this respect. Of course, there have been some major breakthroughs: the developments that stem from Freud; politically, the formulation of our democratic system of government; progressive education. Currently, we have passive resistance, civil disobedience. We also have brain washing of various sorts, some of it coming from the Kremlin, some from Washington, some from Madison Avenue.

As one goes down the list, however, seeking these creative breakthroughs, they seem to be surprisingly sparse, especially when we stack them up against the many serious and unresolved problems that exist today—problems that are steadily increasing and becoming more critical as people become more numerous, more mobile and more facile in communicating with each other and at each other.

I will not explore these. Secretary Hollomon covered many of them in Chapter 1. They include the problems of transportation, pollution, blight, poverty, noise and confusion, mob spirit and mob emotion, the more personal problems of unhappiness or alienation from other people, the problems of mental illness, problems of aging, and so forth. One needs only to list them to recognize we have not come very far.

The question is: What is, or can be, the role of engineering in this situation? One may suggest, first of all, that engineering and the related areas of science and technology have contributed to a considerable extent to the creation of the very problems I am talking about. This being so, the duty rests upon the engineers, as I see it, to help solve them. On the other hand, the engineers cannot do the job alone, any more than the lawyers can solve technological problems without the help of the engineers. This is an area in which there must be cooperation.

The question is not, as C. P. Snow would have it, whether the humanists are insufficiently versed in technology and ought to learn more about it. Nor is it the converse, as many people would suggest, that the technologists don't know enough about the humanities and the social sciences and ought to learn more about them.

The basic point, I am suggesting, is that these groups are all indispensable to one another. They must work together. It is on the basis of this proposition that I urge both the possibility and the desirability of a cross-disciplinary educational effort. Such a step could well bring about, not only the kinds of things that will be discussed by Professor Taylor in the next chapter, but could provide a start toward a type of educational cooperation that could deal successfully with basic and crucial social problems as well.

To put it another way, a program that might start with the limited initial objective of developing more creativity in engineers might produce a spill-over or provide some salutary side effects that could ultimately eventuate in contributions going far beyond that more modest goal.

PART 2

THE CONCEPTS

CHAPTER 4

FACTORS INFLUENCING CREATIVITY

CALVIN W. TAYLOR

ONE of the aims of science and engineering is to make tomorrow more predictable. However, if we study creativity and learn how better to unleash this trait, the chances are that creative individuals will make tomorrow less forecastable because they will come in with even more unexpected ideas, responses, and contributions.

I was once told by an inventor friend that "practically all of the mighty rivers of industry spring from the headwaters of lone wolf inventors or creators." If he is correct, then we should pay attention to these highly important, creative and inventive individuals. We should wonder if our educational systems are producing such people.

I recall an anecdote about John Arnold, one of the pioneers for creativity in engineering education, who had a background in both psychology and engineering. While he was on the faculty at MIT, an interviewer came to him looking for engineers. The person named several characteristics he wanted in these engineers and then Arnold asked him if he hadn't forgotten something, and he said, "No, I don't think so." Arnold said, "Don't you want imagination, too?" He said, "No, I didn't come to MIT for people with imagination. I came for engineers who were technically trained. I didn't expect them to have been trained along imaginative lines." This attitude was one of the things that needled Arnold to investigate the products of the educational system. He spent a large portion of the remainder of his career struggling with the problem of whether education was developing imaginative people or, as the interviewer had suggested, whether you had to look elsewhere for such persons. And he cited some evidence that the latter was more often the picture of what exists.

LIFE HISTORY POWERFUL IN AFFECTING CREATIVITY

Let us first focus upon the formative years—how it all starts—and then move through the formative years to provide a picture of what students are like by the time they reach college and graduate school.

Often any attempt to develop creativity in adults has been called by those who have attempted it remedial in nature—i.e., remedial education. By the time of graduate school, students have been in a "program or pattern of training" for some sixteen years. At the freshman level in college they have been patterned for twelve years and by this time this pattern is fairly strong. If you vary from this pattern in your educational program you will probably run into real resistance from the students, at least from those who are performing best because they don't know where they will stand if the pattern is changed. Consequently, you will have a lot of other habit patterns and resistance to overcome. Chances are that if you do try to get some creativeness in your engineering program during the four years of undergraduate work, it will at first be only a very small proportion of the total emphasis in their college program. So any creative processes and performances may evolve slowly in students who have been educated for sixteen years in a system in which they have had only four years with some part-time attention to creative education, preceded by twelve years in which they are typically and strongly patterned along other lines.

An over-all school environment, certainly during the first twelve years, is many variabled. Probably several of these variables are neutral to creativity, meaning, in effect, that creativity is probably being ignored, neither favored nor unfavored by some of these.

Other variables may have some positive effects on creativity and some others may have negative effects. Over-all, there is no clearcut indication of either a strong positive or a strong negative effect, though there are hints of evidence for each direction. We do know, however, that we certainly do not have an environment that has been built deliberately to be optimum for stimulating or encouraging creativity.

Our present grading system has little validity in predicting later scientific performance, research performance, or engineering activities in research and development. There are at least three cases where the comparison of scores (grades) on the long test that we have called the educational program, and later professional performance in science and engineering, have shown no correlation at all.* In other cases, the correlations are low, but still so low that they do not bear out at all the assumption that grades will forecast creativity to any marked degree. The grading system is not geared to favor creative talent and productive thinking nearly as much as it favors knowledge absorption and regurgitation.

If we look for a moment at the teacher climate—and I am sweeping very broadly with my brush—recent attempts to introduce creative teaching techniques in the classroom suggest that many of our classrooms are taught in an authoritarian manner very much in the way that I am instructing you right now, i.e., I know something you don't know. So I deliver to you as unequivocal, a fact or principle, and expect you, upon my request, to repeat it to me as accepted fact or principle.

When a classroom change is made to a creative teaching technique, it has been found that some students will learn by the creative method more effectively than they would if material were presented in the standard authoritarian way. Others, of course, might be just the reverse. Again, you see, a different group will become star performers as you change the teaching method toward other kinds of talent. We suspect that many more classrooms are employing the authoritarian method rather than encouraging a creative approach.

Not all teachers need to be specialists in creativity, but at some point, early in his schooling, every student ought to be at least exposed to those teachers who employ creative teaching techniques.

We do not suggest that teachers abandon completely the system they are presently using, but rather that they initially experiment with just one or two of these creative techniques while continuing otherwise as they are accustomed to do. We think that the differences they will note in their own and student performance will convince them of the worth of the new things they attempt along creative teaching lines.

At a recent research conference on instructional media and creativity, the instructional media specialists indicated that of all

---

* C. W. Taylor and F. Barron (eds.), *Scientific Creativity: Its Recognition and Development*. Wiley: New York, 1963.

the instructional materials they had produced or had seen, practically none had been designed with creativity in mind.* This indicates two things. First, the instructional media to which students have been exposed at best serves only incidentally to stimulate creative thinking and, secondly, there is an immediate need for the development of instructional media which would serve as a stimulus to creativity.

The interaction among students in the school environment provides a far more powerful factor than is often recognized. There is some evidence that at all ages, certainly among young children just starting school, when you put students together and they start generating new ideas and one of them begins to outstrip the others, interesting reactions occur which tend to stifle the more creative student. The students begin to devise rules which oftentimes turn out to be lasting rules. These rules, if you examine them, tend to be sanctions against certain kinds of performances of individuals showing creative characteristics.

Often, students in this situation tend to say, "We've got to get organized." They then proceed to organize their activities so that the particularly creative individual is appointed a recorder or the like. He is kept busy recording their ideas and he is effectively "organized out of the ball game". Pressures such as this—fear of being either completely controlled or else ostracized by fellow students—have a definite influence on the student.

ARE INQUIRING MINDS BEING DEVELOPED?

A word that is often used in education is "readiness" and the research into this area changes this question. Instead of readiness of the kids for the system, the question that comes up is the readiness of the system for the kids. Especially at younger ages I believe students will rise rapidly to whatever new challenging opportunities we are willing to give them. I will give you a little bit of the feel about this as we go along.

As a student progresses, he grows in practically all things, physically, psychologically, emotionally, and so on. However, during this growth, if you check into some of his thinking abilities, you will find that there are some slumps in thinking abilities. For example, it has

---

* C. W. Taylor and F. Williams (eds.), *Instructional Media and Creativity*. Wiley: New York, 1966.

been shown that fourth graders do not score as high in certain thinking ability tests as third graders. So there is a slump from which there then has to be some recovery and not all people recover equally, nor necessarily to the level forecast if they had not had the slump. I like to think that among the many variables in creativity, certainly in the sciences, one is curiosity or the inquiring mind.

One person, Richard Suchman, who has recently been at the U.S. Office of Education, has been doing what he calls "inquiry training", or teaching high-school students how to ask questions and how to sharpen up each individual question and to have a whole strategy or sequence of questions which are most effective. He has a very definite program where he shows them a scientific phenomenon and then has them try to find an explanation for themselves by using the instructor as a resource person and by asking him questions.

I have asked Suchman why he had to teach youngsters how to ask questions. I thought they did quite well by themselves, but he said, "No, a lot of sharpening can occur in their questioning abilities." So he teaches them to be more effective "prosecuting attorneys" in searching for answers about nature from the instructor.

Later, I saw him give a demonstration of this technique. He shows a short film which displays a scientific phenomenon. After the film it is the responsibility of the students to ask questions; that is, the students have freedom, but also the responsibility to ask questions. In order for his technique to work, the teacher must stand there and do *nothing* until the students start the technique working by asking questions. He said that when he is demonstrating this technique he has had moments of truth (of silence) with *high-school* classes that last for the greater part of the class period before they will start to ask questions.

In the same demonstration with *second graders,* he stated that there is no moment of truth. They immediately start asking questions. So somewhere between the second grade and high school, they have learned how *not* to ask questions, I suspect as a result not only of the attitude of their teachers but of their fellow students as well.

Putting these two together, someone has proposed that a factor in this fourth-grade slump is that this may be about the time when students start learning to ask better questions than the teachers can answer. Perhaps from then on, we teachers teach them how *not* to ask questions.

Let me give you another example on the problem of questioning. One of my friends has done a lot of interesting research at Penn State on the teacher–student relationship in the learning process and the ability of the teacher to help make these processes more or less creative.* One of the things he has done is to go into some college classes and tape-record what happens. Results of his study have shown that in the typical college class he studied there were 40 questions per hour asked. The average time for an answer was something like four seconds. And nearly all of the questions were asked *and* answered by the professor himself.

This is an indicator, I think, that the students really are not encouraged and simply do not have time to do thinking of their own or to develop their own thinking at the rate at which we toss out material to them in many of our courses.

Now on the question of readiness to do research. In teaching the arts, teachers would never dream of doing what has happened in the sciences and in engineering. *In the arts they would never dream of keeping a paint brush away from the student until he was a graduate student.* But in the sciences, by and large, we tell the students to keep their hands off new stuff and to do no new thinking or new experiments of their own.

As an example, let me give you a report about the experience of a high-school student given by a PTA leader in my region. This student won a local Science Fair contest by duplicating a famous experiment. He won the contest and as a reward received trips to the West Coast and Los Alamos, and to West Point and other places on the East Coast. The next year, with greater self-confidence from his success, he decided to strike out on his own and worked in an area requiring some speculative thinking and a little new basic research, and he produced a paper which he submitted in the Science Fair contest. As a result, he was chastized by the judges for "working beyond his province". Whose province did he go beyond? The judges' probably! He didn't get anywhere near the reward for striking out on his own that he got the previous year for following old trails that someone else had carved out. Jablonski has demon-

---

* K. Beittel, Instructional media for creativity in the arts. In C. W. Taylor and F. E. Williams (eds.), *Instructional Media and Creativity,* pp. 277–307. Wiley: New York, 1966.

strated that not only high-school students, but also elementary-school students are remarkably ready to do new scientific research if we will only provide some opportunities and encouragement for them to do so.*

In a study of NASA scientists, we asked them at what times they had learned the most when they were going to school: (a) in the classroom, (b) at home doing their homework, or (c) after school when they were doing something they happened to be interested in at the time. The more creative they had been in their careers, the more often they marked the third choice. So we should resist those who want to lengthen time in classrooms and time doing assigned homework and who thereby would design out any time to be spent on the third choice.

Progress is usually made by those most ready and capable of taking the next step. I once had the experience in Washington of finding the person with the least education most ready to have a new experience by helping me work on a new computer with a visual output.

To make progress in creative kinds of training, we may have to deliberately *not play* into the existing habits, into the existing patterns, into the usual expectations of the students. They may want you to teach the way they have always been taught; so in order to make progress, you may have to go against them.

You may find that you can succeed only by going in a different direction and fighting against the student's natural tendencies, natural only because they have been in the standard system for twelve or more years. The same problems of working against old habits will also emerge when teachers are asked to change their teaching methods.

It is interesting to note that at least two arms of the military service feel that they have succeeded in an electronics training program if they can teach the program in such a way that it destroys any correlation between I.Q. scores and course grades. They have largely succeeded in doing this, which means that they are not trying to have the high I.Q. characteristics be the ones that are functioning while the people are learning the electronics material, but somehow they have other thinking or learning talents

---

* J. R. Jablonski, Developing creative research performance in public school children. In C. W. Taylor (ed.), *Widening Horizons in Creativity*, pp. 203–219. Wiley: New York, 1964.

functioning. Since they have generally not received the more "academically able" (the higher I.Q. students) in the military, it is necessary or at least highly advisable to teach in other ways. They feel they are doing so by destroying this correlation and by refraining from going into the existing habit patterns or usual ways of learning and thinking, and they are having some successes in doing so.

Engineers tend to score high on intelligence tests, especially on the nonverbal mathematical components. But some of these kinds of things are not nearly as highly related to creative performance as we had hoped, though they are related to the typical academic performance. Consequently, I like to make a distinction between what would be called scholarly abilities, in terms of acquiring and mastering man's past knowledge and productive thinking abilities. Psychologically, the task of receiving and reproducing old knowledge is a different process from trying to produce new knowledge by building upon whatever you can. Psychologically, these are different processes and the people who are the star performers as scholars (as masters of old knowledge and reproducers and users of old knowledge) are not necessarily the same as those who are star producers of new knowledge. I suspect strongly that our science education—its books and labs—follows old patterns and rarely allows the student much chance of producing new patterns or new knowledge until at least the seventeenth year in the system, when he has had almost a full year of graduate work.

KNOWLEDGE AND CREATIVITY

I would like briefly to touch on another area, namely, knowledge in relation to creativity. This is a very provocative and troublesome area if you get a group of teachers together. The question really is, what is the role of knowledge or information in relation to creativity? I suspect that we have often almost entirely focused upon the transmission and acquiring of knowledge as the goal of education. We have too often assumed, I think, that if a person becomes full of knowledge, then afterwards all good things will happen to him. But we have a growing suspicion that this kind of transfer of training based upon sheer knowledge does not occur strongly.

Hyman talks about knowledge being both an asset and a liability in creativity.* It is an asset in that it is the building stuff which can be used to go above and beyond the present state of knowledge—out into the unknown. On the other hand, it can be a hindrance in that when you learn existing knowledge you often become so patterned as to put a constraint on your ability to seek unique solutions. The ideal I talk about is to become well versed in knowledge without becoming steeped. To be creative you need to be flexible, but a lot of people seem to lose this. Their knowledge becomes pretty highly patterned and so do they.

Hyman did a two-stage study on two groups. Neither group knew that there would be two stages. In the first stage, both groups were to receive certain information. One group was told to receive it critically and the other group was told to receive it constructively. The first group received this information critically by dealing with it in a very critical way. Later, they had a chance to work on a problem where this earlier information could have been a real asset in the solution of the problem. Those who had taken the critical ("mind set") approach to the problem, by and large, did not use this earlier information as an asset to work on the later problem. In effect, due to their critical approach they had almost rejected the earlier information and didn't have it available for later use.

Those in the second group who received and processed the information constructively found it much easier, apparently, not only to have the information available, but also to use it at a later time when it was pertinent. This was very interesting for, in the whole problem of processing information, you can receive information creatively or not creatively, you can process this information creatively or not creatively, and you can express your ideas, the fruits of your central processes, either creatively or not creatively.

In some of my classes, I have asked students to read the literature and to come up with new ideas of their own they have been sparked to while reading, not ideas that the literature gives them on a silver platter, but ideas that they have been sparked to. In my human engineering class I have also asked them to write a new idea paper for their term paper in which I call for no patent search and no library search. I tell them to come up with a new idea of their own such as a new product, something that is better designed for greater

---

* R. Hyman, Creativity and the prepared mind: the role of information and induced attitudes. In C. W. Taylor (ed.), *Widening Horizons in Creativity*, pp. 69–79. Wiley: New York, 1964.

help to human beings. In both of these types of tasks, the students complain of difficulties because they have never before had an assignment to do something like this. Nonetheless, both the students and I have been very pleased and surprised with the quality of the ideas they can produce if a teacher will give them license and a direct assignment in the official system to do so.

Let us now turn to the problem of knowledge transmission. We are having a great knowledge explosion in science and engineering, so much so that it is estimated that the quantity of information has doubled in the past decade and that the pace will quicken still more. In a recent study we studied nearly a thousand physicians in practice. One of the problems we encountered is that there is no real evidence that the student who is good at gathering knowledge while he is in our artificial educational system or professional college will develop real techniques for keeping abreast of the knowledge after he is on his own. The American Medical Association is now taking a serious look at this in a pilot project in Utah. Our research findings helped to needle them into initiating action on this problem of preparing physicians to keep abreast of this exploding knowledge.

The next question is, to what degree are we learning how to develop students so they will get on the right side of this exploding knowledge? Are we preparing them not only to keep abreast, but even to be party to the producing of this exploding knowledge? To what degree have we done anything in our educational program to prepare them very much for producing new knowledge?

A very interesting challenge is, to what degree do we ever bring into our textbooks or reading materials or classrooms a chance for the students to have experience with the unknown or even to be aware that there are unknowns? What teacher ever says, "You have now read about what is known, so let's talk for an hour about what is not known"? Then the students might see what topics in the text might be exploding in the near future and they can get themselves prepared for their potential role in this world of trying to tackle some of these unknowns. I think we largely keep this area of unknowns hidden from them.

I ask students, "Where do you think your body of knowledge is in relation to the total body of man's knowledge? Where is your knowledge in relation to the fringe of knowledge?" We should all wonder about what kind of a body of knowledge we are giving students. Are they getting out to the fringe of knowledge and having any experience there and maybe even beyond the fringe, out into the unknown?

ARE CREATIVE THINKERS BEING ATTRACTED INTO ENGINEERING?

I contend that, if you check, you will find that there has been very little attention in most of education to the creative process. It is a topic, I think, that has been largely ignored and often overlooked, so that students generally have little knowledge about and few opportunities to experience their own creative process. Hudson at Cambridge, England, has done studies to locate in what fields people who have scored high on thinking tests have decided to major in college. The answer he has found is they are not majoring in the sciences (and I presume that neither are they majoring in engineering). Instead, they are majoring in the liberal arts and humanities, presumably where thinking of one's own is more encouraged.

Let me describe a technique used by James Gallagher of Illinois in the educational setting. Anyone can try this with a group of teachers by saying:

> "Join me in showing certain creative characteristics by thinking flexibly and toying with a problem. Let's flip things over 180 degrees to see how they look from the opposite angle. We are to build the best classroom program possible to accomplish a broad goal. The task is to name each of the *specific features* that you would build into a classroom in order to make it the *best* possible program for the broad goal of *stifling* or *killing* creativity."

After they have thought up 15 or 20 specific features, then innocently ask: "What do all these add up to?" One or more of them is likely to reply that, "it sounds a lot like the program I had when I was in school."

I have written a series of 10 articles entitled "Clues to creative teaching".* In the series I have given numerous leads for teachers to try in their classrooms. For example, one of the things that we

---

* C. W. Taylor, Clues to creative teaching. Series of 10 articles appearing in *The Instructor Magazine,* Sept. 1963 to June 1964, Dansville, New York.

have done is to call for maximizing the thinking, not just maximizing the learning; that is, to have students be thinkers, not merely learners in the classroom.

In a dissertation by W. L. Hutchinson, which I supervised, thinking was to be maximized.* When this was done, at least as much if not more subject matter was learned. Students enjoyed the classwork more. Surprisingly, I.Q. scores correlated at zero with knowledge learned in the classroom program where thinking was maximized. So new persons were the star performers and a new kind of a talented person emerged—the thinking student instead of the learning student, if I may use these analogies. Hutchinson also found that in the traditional classroom, much of the time is spent in instructional procedure. The students would say, "Teacher, exactly what do you want us to do?" and, "Teacher, exactly how do you want us to do it?" So students typically work under close supervision and the teacher does all the thinking and all the planning. The students are deprived of those experiences and are merely learning what the teacher wants them to learn.

Since Hutchinson, as a school principal, trained his teachers to teach in this new way, I argue that deans need to try to do this in their official system and select a few teachers and tell them that they do have permission and should try to elicit productive thinking in their official classroom. If possible, the deans should show them how, as Hutchinson showed his teachers how. I would vote for a variety of attempts in creativity in a classroom and I would vote also for having a severe checkup on whatever is attempted, so that we can see whether it has the effect that we really want.

Dr. Hammond of our own college of engineering at Utah has just received support from the Esso Educational Foundation to do this. They are going to make new attempts for creativity in their educational program, and try a severe checkup to see if creativity has been installed in the classroom.

One of the general findings across research studies is that the more creative the idea a person gets, the more likely he is to be in trouble. I wonder if this would be true in the engineering colleges as well.

A new organization for research on creativity has just been established to extend research on selection, education and the climate

---

* W. L. Hutchinson, Creative and productive thinking in the classroom. Unpbl. doctoral dissertation, University of Utah, 1963.

for creativity. The activities will include the extension of biographical studies and other techniques for selecting and developing creativity to business and industry.*

I like to say that up to the present we have spent much of our time in our classrooms mining for psychological gold. The argument is now let us mine also for psychological uranium. In the missile game, if someone gets a more powerful missile than we have, then we scramble to get an anti-missile missile. Likewise in the creativity game if you examine closely, one type of thing often found a lot is called a killer of creativity. There are many potent killers. So what one then needs is an anti-killer of a killer of creativity. Let me close with a brief story of hope on this. Note the killer that emerges in this story, followed by the anti-killer of the killer.

TOO MUCH CREATIVITY?

At a recent conference one of the participants said, "What if we do decide that creativity is important and we turn our efforts that way the next fifteen or twenty years to do all we can to spot this psychological uranium and develop it in our school program and cultivate it? After about fifteen or twenty years, won't there be too many creative people and won't that be a problem? One or two of them is enough and maybe too many." So here is the killer that comes out, so naturally and powerfully. To this question Lindsey Harmon promptly and brilliantly replied, "Well, if it is a problem, there will be enough creative people around to solve it."

DISCUSSION

BROOKS WALKER: How successful have your students been after having had your type of education? How did they do after they got out?

Doing Well in the System

CALVIN TAYLOR: You are really calling for longitudinal studies which have not yet been done, although they are sorely needed. By and large, there have not yet been many official creativity programs in education of any consequence. So we really do not have an answer at this time. That's why we need a close check-up, whenever so-called creativity programs are attempted, so we can see if they really have any lasting effect and whether that effect is really still on the ultimate target of creativity.

---

* Staffed by my former doctoral students, this nonprofit trusteeship is the Institute for Behavioral Research in Creativity.

DISCUSSION

There is a thing that troubles me about the study by Hutchinson, which I mentioned. He changed the classroom so that the thinkers emerged as the star performers. These were youngsters, at all levels of I.Q. scores, who were in a regular school program. The problem is that after his experiment, these "thinking stars" were thrown back into the regular system, and although they had been star performers for a while in his classrooms, some of them probably fell downwards back in the old system—toward the bottom of the totem pole "where they belonged", since the old system saw only their I.Q. talent. And I think that must have been very discouraging to these "thinking stars", whose period of stardom was terminated when the old system was in effect again.

WILLIAM SHOCKLEY: I was once involved in a ninth-grade science teaching experiment to produce similar results, where the material was quite unstructured and the teachers had a tough time with it. The students who had not been exceptional grade getters performed very well and surprised the teachers. So I think there may be a common phenomenon here.

But I am puzzled by your statement, which doesn't seem to jibe with other things I have heard, that there is an unexpectedly low or even zero relationship between academic and world-of-work performance. I suppose the most noted evidence to the contrary appeared in the data on the "Terman gifted children", where success corresponded with high I.Q.

CALVIN TAYLOR: Good things in people tend to go together slightly, and probably the finding Dr. Shockley mentioned comes out with a low positive correlation. But the correlation isn't anywhere near as high as people think. I know one study at American Telephone and Telegraph in which it appeared from the presentation of their results that there was a high relationship between grades and later performances. But when we checked them out, the highest of their correlations were in the 20's—in the high 20's at best, or maybe 0.30. If you square this correlation of 0.30, you get 0.09, which means you have accounted for 9 per cent of the phenomenon and not accounted for over 90 per cent. So you really do not have a very strong relationship, and there are many, many more unknowns than knowns.

Now I conceive of the "gifted children" in the Terman studies as people who do well in the existing system. They were performing quite successfully in the existing system in school and tended to be above average in "playing the existing ropes well" in later organizations, too. Maybe they also included a slightly above average number of creative people, but they did not necessarily turn out to be creative in general.

Grappling with the Problem

EMANUEL PIORE: There is a growing tide of experimentation in education in almost every field. The approach is two-fold, as I see it. One aspect is to get the curriculum more in terms with the contemporary structure of the subjects, as they are being developed by the senior statesman of each field. The second is to get more involved with the students.

There is a growing urge in this country to come to grips with the problem of how to stimulate young people so that they remain interested, imaginative, and thinking throughout their lives. Some of the best brains in this country are grappling with this problem, and the National Science Foundation and the Office of Education are spending tens of millions of dollars on this work.

CHAPTER 5

NEW DIRECTIONS IN ENGINEERING EDUCATION

WILLIAM BOLLAY

WE HAVE reviewed some of the factors influencing creativity. Let us turn now more specifically to engineering and some techniques for stimulating more innovative thinking during an engineering student's education.

One may question whether there are any general techniques for teaching creative engineering. I believe that there are systematic approaches which can be taught with the aid of illustrative cases. Professor Fritz Zwicky of the California Institute of Technology was a proponent of the "morphological approach" to invention.*
I remember that when he first presented this idea to us in the Navy Bureau of Aeronautics during World War II, there were many of us who were quite skeptical. He asked us to tell him about our problems with jet propulsion, and he promised to bring us some new solutions. He proposed to construct a "morphological box" of all possible methods of solving any problem, looking at it from a very fundamental standpoint. We gave him many problems. We were amazed a couple of months later when he came back to us with the concept which is now called the "pulse-jet" engine. (Unfortunately, the Germans came out a few months later with a fully-developed V-1 pulse-jet.) Needless to say, Zwicky's performance impressed me with the potential of the morphological approach.

A year later Zwicky came up with another new idea as a result of this morphological approach. He said that it was feasible to develop fuels with an efficiency about 30 per cent higher than the traditional hydrocarbon propellants. He did not know at the time whether these fuels should be liquid, solid, or gaseous. Again we

* Fritz Zwicky, *Helvetica Physica Acta* (1950), p. 222. Basel, Switzerland.

took a chance on his ideas and found that the borohydride fuels which he proposed were indeed more efficient. They were not practical competitors for the hydrocarbon fuels from economic and safety standpoints, but these are the kinds of factors that have to be investigated after a *technical* solution has been found. The point is that Zwicky's morphological approach was again demonstrated as a method to find new technical solutions.

More recently, Professor Strong* successfully developed a simplified version of Zwicky's concept which he calls "Modest Morphology". This consists essentially of adding at least *one* new method to the prior art of accomplishing any desired function. By this approach he has been able to achieve an order of magnitude increase in the accuracy of optical gratings.

It is interesting to note that the philosopher René Descartes had started a similar program for invention. He made it his objective to develop rules for invention. Furthermore, he used a technique which might be very useful for developing inventive capability in students. Whenever he heard about an ingenious invention he tried to think through a different way of accomplishing the same objective. By comparing his solutions with that of the inventor he learned to broaden his own approaches.

In talking to many successful inventors I have found that no two follow exactly the same rules. Each has developed his own preferred approach to finding and solving problems. Still, it would be highly instructive to a student to learn about some of these successful techniques, so that he can select those which particularly appeal to him, and thus assemble his own bag of tricks.

I agree with Professor Calvin Taylor that one cannot teach creativity by lecturing about it. One has to get students involved in the process of doing something inventive or innovative. A number of successful teaching techniques have been developed for this purpose. Specifically, the following appear to be good starting points for planning a more extensive program in the future. I shall list them and then discuss each of them briefly.

1. Case histories and case problems.
2. Project laboratories.

* John D. Strong, Introduction to modest morphology, Cal Tech Alumni magazine *Engineering and Science,* May 1964, pp. 18–25.

3. Real experience in the preliminary design of complex systems (by an interdisciplinary, system engineering course at the university).
4. Real experience in industry or government on a part-time basis.
5. Engineering theses on problems requiring significant invention and innovation.
6. Enrichment of science and engineering courses through stimulating examples of the application of theory.
7. Seminars on engineering invention and innovation.
8. Special opportunities for exceptionally creative students.

1. CASE HISTORIES AND CASE PROBLEMS

The case method has been used for many years in teaching law, medicine, and business. This method may also be very useful in engineering education for cultivating judgment, developing motivation in students, and teaching successful methods for invention and innovation. *Case histories* can be used to present to the student some of the methods used by outstanding inventors and innovators in the past. *Case problems* can be used to challenge the student with some unsolved problems on which he can exercise his own skills.

After having studied successful case histories and general principles for invention, I think it is very important that the student has a chance to exercise his ingenuity in the solution of a real problem, to which he does not know the solution. A case problem is, in effect, a statement of the situation faced by an inventor before his invention. The case problem may be a real problem which has been solved but for which the student does not know the solution. Or it may describe a current situation which still requires solution.

Until recently the Department of Commerce used to issue an "Inventions Wanted" list of several thousand problems requiring better solutions. These descriptions were usually too terse to be very useful. A typical aerospace problem, for example, was the following:

> No. 1679: Gravity Gradient Damping for Aerospace Vehicles. Devise mechanisms, such as flexible rods, for conversion of energy so that earth's gravity gradient will serve as a means of dampening and stabilizing an aerospace vehicle.*

---

* *Inventions Wanted by the Armed Forces and Other Government Agencies,* Vol. II, November 1963. National Inventors Council, U.S. Department of Commerce.

At the time this problem was published there were already in existence at least two solutions, one a passive damping method and the other an active damping method. Each of these existing systems had advantages and disadvantages from the standpoint of weight, complexity in erection, reliability, accuracy, and so on. In order for a new system to represent a real advance over these existing systems it would have been necessary to present numerical values on the current state of the art and the targets for an improved system. Only by having such numbers available would it have been possible for an inventive engineer to determine whether he had made an improvement.

Thus, we may conclude that the statement of the case for an unsolved problem needs to be in reasonable detail, including quantitative statements on the current state of the art, and, if possible, a description of the crux of the problem in terms of the most critical aspect for which there is not yet a good solution.

A well-documented case study might, for example, contain the following information:

— A clear statement of the problem.
— A simple discussion of the theoretical and experimental background pertinent to the problem.
— An illustrative numerical example of the theory and an indication of the range of numerical values which are desired, with some indication of the relative worth of achieving these values.
— A discussion of the various approaches tried to date and the quantitative results obtained.
— A discussion by some experts (with names listed) on what they consider the crux of the problems and in which direction there may be promising solutions.
— References to additional literature.

Let me give you an example from the history of gas turbines. During the early 1940's the first practical aircraft gas turbines were developed. Even at that time it was well recognized that a regenerative gas turbine would have a much better efficiency than the simple gas turbine. The U.S. Navy Bureau of Aeronautics initiated the development of a 1000 h.p. regenerative gas turbine at Chrysler sometime around 1944. This program was cancelled a few years later during an economy drive because it appeared that the weight of a heat exchanger of high efficiency was too great to make the regenerative gas turbine very interesting. Now, twenty years later, the regenerative gas turbine development is suddenly being taken up again. What were the new elements responsible for the renewed interest? Principally, two. The first was the development of new technology for forming and welding very thin steel sheets into heat exchangers and, secondly, a recognition that a small diameter passage resulted in a lighter heat exchanger. What could we have done in the 1940's to avoid this delay in innovation? An expert in the gas turbine field could have pointed out these two critical problems. Publicizing this as the crux of the problem for achieving better specific fuel consumptions with a gas turbine than with the conventional piston engine would have attracted the experts in the neighboring technologies of materials and heat transfer to this important problem.

Among the current unsolved problems, for example, is a method for measuring and recording the mean atmospheric parameters from a satellite. In this case, constant pressure Mylar balloons carrying miniaturized instrumentation are one possible answer; however, the thin film batteries which are distributed over the surface of the mylar are currently very unsatisfactory. By describing the total problem, including the most critical aspect—in this case the thin film battery—a student of chemical engineering could possibly make an important invention by conceiving a better method of constructing this battery. On the other hand, a student of electrical engineering may propose an entirely different system, such as, for example, a balloon carrying only a corner reflector and measuring the wind velocity by a doppler measurement from the satellite. Or an instrumentation engineering student might develop an improved microwave radiometer which makes feasible completely remote probing from the satellite. The statement of the case should therefore include a statement of the overall system objectives as well as the critical aspects of the various solutions which have been tried.

An accurate and complete statement of a case problem involving the need for innovation would represent a suitable task for a master's thesis; moreover, it would be excellent experience for a young engineer to assemble this kind of background data which normally forms the first step in a new engineering development.

Such well prepared case study statements might form the subject either for a student thesis or, in the case of simpler problems, for a classroom assignment. The National Bureau of Standards is currently considering a program to encourage the development of such case studies by the various government departments which have an interest in science and technology.

2. PROJECT LABORATORIES

The "project laboratory" is a very successful instrument for stimulating students to be inventive. I had an opportunity to observe such a laboratory at the Department of Aeronautics at the Massachusetts Institute of Technology and was very much impressed with the motivating influence of the laboratory upon the students. It gives junior and senior students an excellent experience in the design, construction, test and evaluation of a *simple* device of their own choosing. The device must cost less than $100, and thus must be kept simple. The project laboratory involves one engineering experience in depth on a narrow problem. In contrast, a design course utilizing cases of the type I have described may cover 20 or 30 situations involving invention and innovation. Thus, these two techniques, the design course and the project laboratory, are complementary.

3. REAL EXPERIENCE IN THE PRELIMINARY DESIGN OF A COMPLEX NEW ENGINEERING SYSTEM

A university course of this kind is best carried out by a multidisciplinary team of students of engineering, science, business, and the social sciences. The course requires the cooperation of a number of faculty members representing various fields of engineering, as well as lectures from industry in order to present the state of the art. Such system engineering studies have been carried out during the past four years at MIT and Stanford University at the senior and graduate levels. By undertaking system engineering studies of complex systems which have not yet been studied by industry, it has been possible for the student teams to come up with significant new innovations. The new ideas generated by such studies have also served to guide graduate students toward more fruitful areas for their master's and doctor's research.

4. REAL R & D EXPERIENCE AS AN INDUSTRIAL INTERN OR "COOP" OR PART-TIME STUDENT

Probably the best technique for learning creative engineering is real experience with imaginative engineers and scientists who are working on exciting R & D problems at the frontiers of technology.

This experience can be obtained on a part-time internship basis either on major R & D projects at the university (such as the MIT Instrumentation Laboratory or the Jet Propulsion Laboratory of Cal Tech) or at a nearby industrial or governmental laboratory. This latter possibility is available, for example, to students at Stanford, who work part-time in companies such as Lockheed or in the NASA Ames Laboratory. The ideal internship experience is one which permits a student to participate over a number of years on a real development project through all of its phases from design to construction, test, and evaluation, including the real constraint of delivering a product on schedule.

Most U.S. engineering schools do not have such internships open to a large number of students. Thus it is desirable that design and project courses be made available to larger numbers of other engineering students. These courses can start with simple design projects in the freshman year and lead up to relatively sophisticated projects for master's and doctor's theses.

5. ENGINEERING DESIGN THESES

There is ample precedent to show that university-based projects can profoundly stimulate a student to make a major creative contribution. The turbo-jet engine was invented independently by Frank Whittle at Cambridge University, England, and by Hans von Ohain at the University of Göttingen, Germany. Similarly, Werner von Braun performed his Ph.D. thesis at Berlin in physics (1934) on liquid rocket propulsion. Frank Malina obtained his Ph.D. at Cal Tech in 1940 under Dr. Theodore von Karman with a thesis on rocket design and experimentation. Malina's experiments and design of rockets led to the now famous Cal Tech Jet Propulsion Laboratory and to the formation of the Aerojet General Company. These examples indicate that university-based design projects and theses can be, in every way, as creative as theoretical research projects. Ph.D. theses in engineering design should therefore be encouraged.

6. ENRICHMENT OF SCIENCE AND ENGINEERING COURSES THROUGH STIMULATING EXAMPLES OF THE APPLICATION OF THEORY

Source material can be collected suitable for supplementary lectures or problems in the standard courses in physics, chemistry, and the various engineering sciences to stimulate imaginative thinking among the students. This source material might include subjects such as the following:

(a) Interesting engineering devices which illustrate the application of fundamental principles, particularly recently developed ones which are not yet in the textbooks. The source material may be in the form of printed material or models, pictures, slides, or films. (*Example:* The use of a "Yo-Yo" for despinning a satellite, as an illustration of the principle of angular momentum.)

(b) The history of the development of the device in question, including the state of the art before the development.

(c) Interesting anomalies which illustrate the need for extreme care in the application of scientific principles. (*Example:* The Hilsch vortex tube, which was thought by some people to violate the Second Law of Thermodynamics.)

(d) Engineering failures, and an analysis of what might have been done to anticipate and avoid them. (*Example:* Pump cavitation resulting in violent longitudinal oscillation of a liquid fueled missile booster.)

(e) Frontier regions in which engineering applications have not yet been well developed—for example, at extremely low or high temperatures, low or high pressures, and so on.

This source material could be woven into orthodox lectures, or used in special lectures to supplement the traditional lectures on engineering and the sciences.

7. SEMINARS ON ENGINEERING INVENTION AND INNOVATION

Schools of engineering and science should be encouraged to start seminar programs on engineering invention and innovation. Such a seminar might go far to maintain and stimulate the inventive thinking of students of science and engineering. It might be offered each year as an elective, designed to match the increasing technical competence of the student as he advances in his studies. Some of the topics which might be appropriate for such a seminar are the following:

(a) An interesting new technological development, including some background on the innovator and how the development was accomplished.
(b) Discussions by successful engineering innovators of their methods, illustrated by examples.
(c) Methods for finding important problems which yield to solution.
(d) Methods for stimulating creative thought processes and group innovative techniques.
(e) Methods for developing and selling an invention.
(f) Methods for overcoming resistance to innovation.
(g) Fundamentals of patents and how to utilize the patent literature as an informational source.
(h) Histories involving failures in invention and innovation and explanations of the failures.
(i) Means for finding new uses for existing discoveries (solutions in search of problems).
(j) Governmental activities relating to invention and innovation.
(k) Interesting inventions by local faculty and students.
(l) Exhibits and discussions of designs and experimental projects carried out by students.
(m) Rewards that follow successful new product development.

8. SPECIAL OPPORTUNITIES FOR EXCEPTIONALLY CREATIVE STUDENTS OF ENGINEERING

The psychologists are not yet able to identify that one-tenth of one per cent of the engineers and scientists who really will come up with the break-throughs in technology. However, I think it is not very difficult for any professor to find out within which five per cent of his class these really inventive students are located. Special courses and projects should be made available for these students. If we could provide special opportunities to this five per cent of our engineering students who appear to have superior talent for invention and innovation, I think we might achieve the greatest impact on future generations of creative engineers.

Unfortunately, in engineering we have a situation a little different from that in science. If you ask the question, "What have been the hundred most important scientific research findings during the last year?" you would probably find that a very high percentage of the scientists who came up with these are at universities. If you ask another question, namely, "What have been the hundred most significant inventions and innovations during the last year?" you would find that probably very few of these have been made by people at universities. Most of the highly inventive engineers are in industry. Many design departments at universities include staff members who have never directly participated in any major or significant engineering design. Somehow we should try to bring the outstanding inventors and innovators together with the highly creative engineering students at the universities.

I think that this would be a meritorious program for some foundation, and I would like to conclude by suggesting a program along the following lines:

—Selecting in each field of engineering the most significant innovations which have been made during the year and identifying, in each case, the one or two individuals most directly responsible for the engineering innovation.
—Honoring the top 100 of these outstanding innovators by a National Award of $1000 each. The distribution of awards among the fields of engineering might be based upon the respective numbers of professional engineers working in the various fields. In turn, the awards in each field might be apportioned among the major activities therein according to the number of engineers participating in the various activities.
—Inviting these 100 outstanding engineering innovators to devote about a half-day, twice per week, to supervise project or design activities of the most creative 5 per cent of the engineering students. In this manner about 1500 engineering graduates per year would have an opportunity of directly studying with great engineering innovators.

The cost of such a program would be quite nominal. Assuming a foundation would provide an honorarium of $200 per day to these 100 outstanding engineering innovators, the cost of a 30-week program at the rate of one day per week would be $600,000 per year. Hopefully, the universities which would be the beneficiaries of such a program would be willing to continue this consulting arrangement with the award winner during the following years and arrange for a visiting professorship if the cooperation was mutually satisfactory. These visiting professors would not devote their time to giving lectures about creativity but would advise the students on their designs or projects in much the same way as a professor doing research directs the work of his graduate students.

DISCUSSION

ROBERT A. CHARPIE: I doubt that finances are in any sense an important question regarding the availability of the industrial inventors and innovators you're looking to bring into a university two afternoons a week. Identifying these individuals and getting them made available is a problem independent of financing. If you work on financing you are working on the wrong end of the problem.

L. M. BOELTER: You mentioned, Dr. Bollay, that in your experience of presenting students with very complex problems in preliminary design, they do as well as industrial people. How do you explain this?

WILLIAM BOLLAY: The students are less inhibited in looking at unconventional solutions than most professional engineers. Of course, they lack experience and, thus, it will usually take them a little longer to work out a design solution or to make technical decisions.

Another key factor in facilitating such system engineering projects at the university was that we were able to obtain state of the art reports and lectures from many of the leading engineers in industry and government. Many of these speakers were willing to contribute their time to a university, but might not have been available to a competing industrial organization.

CHAPTER 6

THE PROCESS OF INVENTION

JACOB RABINOW

It is fitting that I expound on the process of invention in relation to education, because I flunked every expository course I took in college, and upon graduating at the beginning of the Great Depression and trying to become a teacher in New York City, I flunked all the competitive exams.

Let me begin by asking what appears to be a rhetorical question: How much creativity does the world really want? We take the need for creativity as a matter of faith. We assume people want more and more creativity—more new art, music, poetry, inventions, everything.

I have asked several economists if there is any limit to the amount of creativity that is good for a nation. The experts are not sure. They think that there isn't enough in the United States, that other countries seem to have more. We hear the experts say that creativity is rising at a rate of some 3 to 6 per cent per year, depending on how you slice the statistics. But the question is, how much is good? Is 100 per cent good? Obviously not, because we would obsolete our equipment faster than we could use it. Is 20 per cent good? 3 per cent? 6 per cent?

It may be true that we do not need much more creativity although, as an inventor, I certainly hope we do. In any case, the question of how much creativity we want has a direct bearing on what society offers in the way of inducements to inventors and other creative people. It is reflected in the way we educate people and in the way we reward their behavior.

SOCIETY AS A MASS

I think of society, as a whole, as a kind of ponderous mass. This is also true of business, government, and the universities as subsystems. You try to sell a new idea and you find you are fighting tremendous inertia. This inertia means that the social system has a built-in lag. Electrical engineers know that the presence of mass results in a lagging system and that no matter how hard you drive it, it always succumbs to the force a little late.

The job of the inventors is to provide the lead for a lagging system. We are supposed to recognize needs ahead of the rest of society, to see how to do things before society is quite ready to do them. This is the penalty of being an inventor. If you invent something when everybody wants it, it is too late; it's been thought of by everybody else. If you invent too early, nobody wants it just because it is too early. If you invent very late, after the need has passed, then it is just a mental exercise. I assure you that it is very hard to invent just at the right time.

We inventors therefore have to push individuals and companies and governments into doing things and using things before they are ready, and if we push hard enough against the social lagging network, maybe things work out about right. In my more sober moments I think we don't come out quite even, but we do get someplace.

Now this inertia is, in a sense, a good thing. Society's inertia acts like a built-in filter. It cuts out some of the "baloney" that inventors like to dish out. We inventors love new ideas for their own sake, and if you listen carefully to us, you'll find that a great many ideas aren't worth implementing. Often this is because they weren't thought through to the end, or they weren't tested thoroughly, or there wasn't enough time. In any case, while I detest most of the inertia I have to fight, I have to admit that, when I am on the other end of the scale and ideas are submitted to me, I often have to take a questioning and critical attitude. The ideas have to be proved, and it is usually very difficult to prove in advance that a new idea is good.

THE NATURE OF INVENTION

By what process does one invent? There are big differences of opinion on the subject. I believe inventors invent in a completely random fashion. In order for a computer to do the same thing, it would have to be provided a program by which it could try things without knowing where it is going and evaluate each new and unexpected result. It's as if you put on cards all the knowledge you have in your brain, throw the cards into the air, and then look at the arrangement after they all fall down. Sometimes you may get something new.

I don't believe one can truly invent logically. I have tried to find out what a "morphological" approach is, and I have never gotten a straight answer. I have heard people tell me that the way to invent is to take all the known facts, put them in a logical order, and the answer will be apparent. To this, all I can say is "Bunk." Occasionally, we do approach things logically and get logical answers, and we even get patents on the logical answers. But these are not the great inventions. These are not—forgive me for the expression—"flashes of genius".

What you have to do in mating new ideas is to try to put together things which you don't know in advance will go together. In other words, if you can do something logically, you can program a computer to do it, or you can have a group of people do it. But the good inventions aren't made this way. I'll try to give you some examples.

The best article I've ever read in this connection was written by Bill Shockley.* This was a study of a peculiar phenomenon of human nature. In it Shockley says that in most particulars human beings are about equal. The average runner, in decent health, can run perhaps 50 per cent slower than a champion; we can all memorize about the same amount; or we can lift about the same weight. We are about equal in most abilities, but not in creativity. Here Shockley finds the differences are very, very large. He studied several laboratories, Bell Laboratories, the National Bureau of Standards, and others, and he found each contained one or two men with a great many patents. Some men had a few each and, finally, there was just a scattering. He found that this is so in all creativity—in music there are a few who write great music, and a great deal of it, and then the curve falls off.

Shockley surmised that creativity must not have a simple functional relationship to the workings of the brain; if it did, it would be more or less equal among most people. He postulated that if an invention requires the combination of four ideas, and a man can

---

* William Shockley, On the statistics of individual variations of productivity in research laboratories, *Proceedings of the IRE*, March 1957, pp. 279–290.

put the four together, he may get it. A man who can only put together three ideas at a time will never get it. And so, Shockley analyzed this phenomenon mathematically and showed that if a man can put together twelve ideas, and a second can do only six, he's not just twice as good as the second fellow; he's some hundred or a thousand times better. Consequently, Shockley concluded that small differences in the idea-associating abilities of individuals make a tremendous difference in their creativeness.

Inventive ability is dependent upon how many ideas one can put together at one time. I think this is also true of poetry. One has words in his head, tries different combinations and picks those that sound poetic. Perhaps you can get a computer to try all the words in the English language, but its selections won't be very good compared to those of a human being.

I imagine musicians write music by a random process. They try notes mentally or play them on a piano to see how they sound, and then select those which sound good together. I think this is the way all creative processes have to be done—by random trial and error. I don't think creativity can be approached in any other way. I may be wrong, but I can't imagine anybody writing great music by a logical process. I've observed people compose music; they try and discard, try and discard, and if they are very good at it, they try a great many times.

This means, if the theory is correct, that the amount of information you have available to play with is most important. I disagree with those who say that too much knowledge is bad for an inventor because it biases him. It may indeed, but I think that without a great number of facts, one can't invent. I recall that Kettering once said that education is bad for a man because it teaches him too many things that he can *not* do. This may be partially true, but I think education has two facets, (1) the things it teaches you, and (2) what it teaches you to do with them. I think that education is absolutely necessary, for otherwise people would invent the same things over and over again. You must know what has been done by others in your field : indeed, in quite different fields as well. From this knowledge you have to conceive combinations that other people have never thought of, and I submit that this must be done by a crazy random process—by pure luck, if you like.

TRY EVERYTHING

It is very difficult to explain to people about the number of trials you have to make, how often you beat your brains out, and try one thing after another. Either you discard the results because you are a severe critic of your own ideas, or your friends demolish them because they are more severe than you are. But you keep trying and eventually you may get something that goes together. And if it doesn't go together, you've got to try another technique which I call the "606" approach. This is to try everything, and see what works. During the war we had some tough problems, and when we couldn't come up with bright ideas, we just tried everything. It is not a very cheap way of solving problems, but it did produce Salversan and other things. When I use it, I consider this method somewhat degrading. I do it because a customer wants something, and I have no clear way of doing it, except trying everything; so I do.

I think Edison used the "606" approach in his search for a satisfactory filament. He even tore hairs out of the beards of his visitors, so the story goes. He tried everything until he found the carbon filament. Most of the time, of course, Edison didn't have to resort to this—he was far too bright. But it's a workable method; if you have to tear hair out of a visitor, and the hair works, the process is just as good as getting an idea out of thin air.

FIX IT BUT DON'T CHANGE IT

Let me give you some examples of my approach to invention to illustrate some of the points I have tried to make. Concrete examples, especially simple ones, are better than talking in generalities.

A man came to me once and said, "I have a problem." This is the opening sentence of many visitors. "I have a gadget that arms a bomb after the propeller turns a few hundred times. A screw moves out of a hole and the bomb goes into the armed condition. My problem is that the girls tighten the screws too much and the propeller can't start turning. The air stream isn't strong enough, when the bomb is falling, to make the screw turn. Give me a simple way to stop a girl from tightening the screw too much."

I said, "Simple! There is a whole class of mechanisms that pre-

THE PROCESS OF INVENTION

vent a screw from turning more than a fixed number of times. For example, a set of stacked washers and other such devices will do this."

He said, "If I wanted to use a standard mechanism I wouldn't come to you. You are supposed to be a bright guy who can fix the fuse without changing anything." This is another expression that inventors hear often: "Fix it, but don't change a thing!"

So I said, "Well, let me think about it." This meeting was at my home and I suddenly got an idea. I went downstairs and got a Shake-Proof lock washer. It's a washer that goes on the screw to prevent it from loosening. It has teeth all around, bent in such a way that as you tighten the screw, the teeth jam and the screw locks in position. I softened this lock washer in a gas flame over the kitchen stove, turned the teeth the other way and now I had a very interesting washer, which my wife called the "unlock washer". Now, you couldn't tighten the screw, but you could loosen it very easily. I was very proud of this device. Then the question was, could I get a patent, and the answer was, "No." They already sell left-handed lock washers. I was very proud of the washer. It's very easy to design a guided missile system, but it's quite another thing to invent a new lock washer. Try it.

I would like to point out that this kind of invention can't be done by a logical approach. Perhaps there is a kind of inverting logic that we can at times use: "Let's try it backwards." Why should I have done that to a lock washer? Well, one can see that there's a connection between a screw and a washer and that's how the idea is born. One begins to think of all the things one knows about screws, or about things that have something to do with screws. One thinks of a washer, then a backwards lock washer, and suddenly everything fits.

I'd like to tell you about another trivial invention, because I'm proud of the trivial ones. It's like loving more those children who have the greatest problems. I'd like to tell you about a speed reducer that no one ever used commercially. The problem, again, was in connection with ordnance. We were developing a rocket fuse during World War II. The fuse had a pre-wound spring that drove a little escapement, a clockwork so arranged that a few seconds after firing the rocket the fuse was armed. The Air Force wanted us to design a mechanism into the fuse so that if it didn't hit a target within a few more seconds after firing (it was an air-to-air missile) the rocket was to destroy itself. And the interesting limitation was stated again: "The device is in production; don't change anything, but give us the new feature of self-destruction at the end of x seconds."

So, I invented a speed reducer. I needed something which had to fire the detonator at the end of ten turns of the arming escapement and explode the rocket. Let me describe the invention.

A helical spring drives a wheel attached to the end of a spring. The wheel drives a clock. (We were asked not to add anything to this basic mechanism, which was already a part of the fuse.) Now, if you wind this spring ten turns and watch the spring unwind, you'll notice a very interesting action. The end of the spring that is fixed stands still, while the end attached to the wheel makes ten turns. The middle section of the spring, during this time, will make five turns. The section one-tenth of the way from the fixed end will make one turn and so on along the spring. Thus, if you attach a contact to the spring one-tenth of the way from the fixed end, the contact will make one revolution while the clock-driving end makes ten revolutions. By fastening such a movable contact to the spring and providing a corresponding stationary contact on the frame, I had the necessary mechanism to fire the fuse at the end of the desired period. This device is a speed reducer which is not good for anything else. As you see, it is not really a good gadget, but I am very proud of it.

Again, how does one do this logically? By what logical process can you look at a fuse clockwork and decide that you can get a speed reducer out of the spring itself? Since the time when this was conceived, I found one other mechanism that resembles this clock spring. I had never noticed this device before. It's curious, but once you think of a mechanism, you can easily recognize its relatives elsewhere. I'm not particularly proud of designing the first guided missile control system because that was a lot of different hardware put together. Perhaps some parts of the assembly were quite clever, but most of it was just assembled in a conventional manner. I'm much more proud of the spring speed reducer.

SHORT LETTERS ARE MUCH HARDER

I want to tell you about another gadget, again trivial, because it illustrates particularly well how an inventor works. In this case

THE PROCESS OF INVENTION

I was very conscious of the process of invention. My patent attorney and I were driving from Cleveland. We had just demonstrated a good headlight dimmer, a safety device which the automobile industry didn't want because it cost an extra dollar. Anyway, we were driving back to Washington.

My friend said to me, "Jack, I have a problem. I subscribe to an answering service, and when I'm out of the office they take messages. Every time I come back to the office I have to call them to find out whether there's a message. Often I forget, and that's the time when there is a message. If I call and there is no message, I waste their time and mine. Can you build me something so that when my phone rings it will turn on a light and I will know there is a message?" I said, "Well, that's simple. Take a microphone and a two-stage audio amplifier, put a latching relay on the output, and connect a light to the relay." He said, "Look, if I wanted to use an audio amplifier and a latching relay, I don't need you; I'm an electrical engineer, myself. I want something simple."

"Well," I replied, "if you want something simple and cheap, it will require more thought." There's a famous story about President Lincoln having written a very long letter to a friend, and the friend later asking how the beleaguered President had time to write such long letters. The President replied that he did not have time to write short ones.

Anyway, as we were driving back to Washington, a solution occurred to me. When I came to America in 1921 (I was eleven years old), I saw a toy and that toy was the answer to the telephone problem. A small celluloid dog was placed into a small cardboard dog house. If you clapped your hands, or yelled, "Rex," the dog jumped at you. The mechanism consisted of a battery and a magnet, and at the back of the box were two contacts against which lightly rested a hanging pendulum. As the back of the box was vibrated by a loud sound, the circuit became intermittent, and the magnet released a spring which caused the dog to jump. The whole thing sold for a half-dollar.

I had remembered the toy dog after a lapse of some thirty-five years, and I said to my friend, "I know how to make your telephone device very cheaply." When I came home, I built a contact that opened easily when vibrated. To this I connected a neon light which has a curious characteristic that can make it stay lighted once

81

it is triggered. I gave the gadget to my friend and showed him that it could be easily built for less than a dollar.

He called me back a day later and said, "Yes, I have it on my desk and you're still a lousy inventor." I said, "What's the matter now?" He said, "I can't sneeze, I can't close the door, I can't even open a window because of the traffic noise." So, we incorporated a time delay into it so that the sound had to last for at least two seconds. I obtained a patent on the device, but about the same time the telephone company came out with a device that lights a red light whenever your phone rings. You can now get it as standard equipment and you don't need my silly gadget.

A RUSSIAN MEMORY STORE

I mention this episode because I believe it illustrates a significant point. I once told this story at an information retrieval meeting and was told that it is perfectly obvious what went on in my brain. It went back and looked up an index entitled "Sound-operated devices". Then it went through the file and found "A toy dog". My answer was: "Now that's very interesting, except that in 1921 I had no way of knowing that some silly patent attorney would ask me, some thirty years later, for a sound-operated device." If I were filing the toy dog, I'd file it under "Toys", "Dog", "Rex", but certainly not under "Sound-operated devices". Moreover, there's a more difficult problem. I spoke only Russian when I came to the United States and I would have had to file it under a Russian listing. I don't think my brain could have translated my whole memory into English. In general, there's no way of filing things under the titles or in the order in which you're going to need them later. This is why, when I hear people talk about automatic retrieval of significant information in the Patent Office, I believe they are talking nonsense. You can certainly set up automatic retrieval of trivial information. Until computers can file things without any order of preference, and not know in advance what is important and what is not important about a subject, and until they are able to look up the information later in any order and in any context, including by pictures, smell, and sound, we shall not have creative machines. I don't say this will not be done some day, but not in the immediate future.

The difficulty is this: The human brain apparently can remember our experiences, whether they are smells or sounds or pictures, and the brain can "re-live" them later. We have all had the experience of smelling something and saying, "I smelled this thirty years ago under some specific circumstances," and then the whole scene flashes back. The inventor must have this ability to search through everything he has ever experienced that may have some bearing on a problem, and extract the needed items out of this peculiar thing we call the brain. The items are recalled in connections which were not foreseeable because there's no way of foreseeing now what one will need in the future.

Perhaps people like myself have a warped intelligence. For example, I can't remember the names of people. I meet them and two minutes later I can't introduce them to anyone else. This is a useful thing to tell audiences; then I'm not so embarrassed later on. I really am very poor at it. Someone I know says I don't like people, but that's not true. I happen to like people; I just can't remember their names. I can, however, remember technical things without any effort at all.

ASKING THE RIGHT QUESTIONS

Let me relate to you a few other samples of the kind of thinking one does when one invents. I once conceived an idea of which I'm very proud and, again, which nobody wants. This is a process of taking blurred photographs and later de-blurring them. You may laugh, but the Air Force spends big money on this sort of thing. I took a picture of the New York skyline with a Leica while riding across one of the bridges. The picture has a slight vertical blur because it was taken late in the evening. The exposure had to be quite long even with an F-2 lens. I had it hanging in one of our rooms and as I was sitting across the room and looking at it, I was saying to myself, "It looks good as an eleven by fourteen enlargement, but I know it's blurred vertically." No one noticed this but it bothered me. Having nothing to do—I often have nothing to do, because I'm lazy—I began to wonder whether one could remove the blur from a blurred picture without "fudging", that is, by rigorous processing.

Once I asked the right question, the wheels began to turn, and the answer was "Yes." It seemed a rather straight-forward process, although the mathematics of it are too much for me. David Gilbarg, who is head of the math department at Stanford, later did the theory. He pointed out that a blur is a type of an integration process and that by taking the correct derivatives one can almost always solve the problem of deblurring, providing certain boundary conditions are present.

The problem interested me because it illustrated the kind of invention which I like, one which nobody asked me for. You're not sure there's any good reason for it, but suddenly you begin to question "Can it be done?" And when you ask the question, the solution follows. One of the big tricks in inventing is not so much to invent the "how", but the "what". In other words, the creating of the problem is as big an invention as the solving of the problem—sometimes, a much greater invention.

Many years ago I invented a magnetic clutch and it received considerable publicity and I received many invitations to speak. This is why I can do it now without dying a thousand deaths, as I did before the clutch. One of the talks was before the Optimists' Club of Washington. A man came to me afterwards and said, "I'm head of the biggest diaper wash service in Washington. We'd like to be able to count them without opening them." I didn't ask him why. He asked, "Is this a difficult problem?", to which I said, "Medium." I suggested that they sew into the corner of each diaper a small bead of metal, then X-ray the batch of diapers from two directions. From the resulting picture we should be able to tell how many diapers there are in the bag. He thought that my suggestion was too sophisticated a solution for his unsophisticated business. As far as I know, nothing was ever done with it. The point is that once the problem is posed, most competent engineers will think of some kind of solution. They will vary from brilliant to stupid, but they will be solutions.

RE-INVENTING THE WHEEL

When I came to Washington, nearly thirty years ago, I thought of a stereo motion picture system. I went to the Patent Office Search Room and told an attendant that I was going to look for the idea. He said, "That's multiplex photography. Don't bother looking. Since you work at the Bureau of Standards and they're part of the Department of Commerce, as we are, go directly up to the Examiner in Chief. He'll help you find it."

THE PROCESS OF INVENTION

I found the division and the right examiner. He sat in a small office surrounded by little drawers, called "shoes", which were full of patents in his particular art. I explained to the venerable gentleman that I had a system of three-dimensional movies where one eye sees the odd pictures and the other eye the even pictures as the successive pictures are projected on the screen. I had a revolving shutter in front of the face of the viewer to select the pictures. The examiner listened and then, without looking, picked up a patent and said, "Like this?"—and there was my invention, with my exact drawing, dated 1910, the year I was born. I never got over the shock. What left me thunderstruck was that the drawing was identical with my sketch. If I hadn't seen the date, I would have sworn that the other inventor stole it from me.

INVENTION BY ANALOGY

Some of my inventions have made money and are important—at least, economically. One is the magnetic particle clutch for which I received immense rewards—a gold medal from the Department of Commerce, and a steep raise in salary. As a result of this I was making more money than my boss, which raised many non-technological problems. Anyway, the clutch invention came about in a curious way. There was an accidental discovery of an electrostatic particle clutch by a man named Winslow when he was playing with a Johnson–Rhabek clutch. I won't give you the whole history of clutches. Winslow was playing with another clutch and discovered a curious effect: if particles of starch or limestone were embedded in a film of oil between two plates and if he applied a high voltage across the mixture, the particles chained up into a kind of conglomerate that made the two plates bind together. He applied for a patent on this device and the Patent Office, of course, rejected it as unworkable. So he came down to the Patent Office in Washington and demonstrated the electrostatic clutch and got the patent. The patent was tested at the Massachusetts Institute of Technology. They played with it and didn't like it very much. It finally reached one of the consulting firms to my group at the National Bureau of Standards. On one occasion, while playing with it in our lab, it suddenly occurred to me that if electrostatic attraction could be made to do the job, electromagnetic attraction should be very much better. The Mu of iron is about a thousand or two thousand, while the K of starch is about two, so that for the same field stress, if you like, one should be able to get a thousand times more sheer force. Besides, one doesn't have high voltage problems, and a lot of other things should be easier.

So we tried it, and about an hour later we had the first magnetic particle clutch. And then the roof caved in. Apparently, clutches had been a pain in the neck for a long, long time. Apparently, they still are. This was the first new, efficient, different clutch in many years. It didn't wear out, didn't need adjustments and had several other virtues.

The U.S. patent rights were vested in the U.S. Government, while I retained the foreign rights. I mention this because people have often asked me, "How many millions did you make on the magnetic clutch?" In the United States I earned nothing but a grade step raise and a lot of glory, and I learned how to speak in public, after a fashion. After five years of great effort and forty-four foreign patents in twenty-two foreign countries, I earned a little over twenty thousand dollars. That is the total.

However, the feeling of accomplishment was very sweet. Very many people knew about the clutch, and to this day people talk about it. It has become a familiar, commercially available device. It found its way into the Hillman car, the Peugeot, the Renault. It is used in many IBM machines and in all Control Data tape drives. But I must say that even engineers in my own company don't know that I invented it.

The clutch illustrates the "invention by analogy" method. Inventors do this very often. The Patent Office is sometimes unsophisticated enough to issue patents when one invents something by using analogous art. If it's "too analogous", they won't let one get away with it, but if it's not obviously analogous, one can get away with it. This is one of the tricks patent attorneys pull out of their hats. What surprised me in the particular case of the particle clutch is that it wasn't done before me. I had occasion to tell of the clutch to J. Presper ("Press") Eckert, who is one of the inventors of the electronic digital computer—you may remember the Eckert and Mauchly Corporation. He thought a minute and said, "You know, Jack, I have an idea for another invention. I can make an electrostatic clutch similar to your gadget." "Press, you just closed the loop," I said, and told him about Winslow's original electrostatic clutch. Here you see Press, a very brilliant inventor, doing exactly

THE PROCESS OF INVENTION

what all inventors do. They immediately start beating their brains out to see if they can improve on what you just said. After a while this becomes a way of life. You see something that bothers you or interests you, and you invent.

THERE MUST BE A BETTER WAY

My automatic watch regulator was another useful invention. If you have an American car with a clock in it, you've paid me three-quarters of a cent because all American car clocks use it. Now, if the clock doesn't run, that's not my fault. But if it runs incorrectly, that *is* my fault, and I'll give you back the three-quarters of a cent.

It all began in 1945, when my wife gave me a present of a Gruen wrist watch. It was a good watch and waterproof, too. Have you ever tried to adjust a waterproof watch? You just unscrew the back, but you need a special tool. And if you don't have the tool, you wreck the case. Nevertheless, you unscrew the back and you find the gadget marked "F" and "S" (fast and slow) and you move it a little bit in the right direction. The correct amount is a "little bit", but the correct amount varies and no one knows how much is correct. You just move the F–S lever a little bit, depending on your eyesight. Then you screw the cover back on, if you can. After wearing it a while, you discover that it's now adjusted a little too far, so you open it again and move it "half a little bit" in the other direction. Finally, if you're very careful and don't get dirt into the watch and don't hurt the mechanism, you get it regulated. For six months you have a good watch and then it starts drifting in some other direction, because by now it's winter. The average temperature is lower, so the oil inside is a little thicker, or thinner, or dryer. After having done this for about a year, being an inventor, I said, "Nuts to this! There must be a better way." And so I invented the self-regulating watch. I'm wearing one of them. When you pull at the stem and move the hands forward, the rate speeds up a little. If you move them back, the rate slows down. In a clock this is a very simple device. It makes the clock actually cheaper and better because it eliminates the regulating stem and the act of regulation, which most people can't perform anyway.

The device is actually a form of an integrating servo system. This I didn't know when I invented it, but people pointed it out to me later. You know, most inventions are later analyzed by the theoreticians, and people enjoy explaining to us what it was that we really did, and why it was obvious.

IMPROVING PERFECT WATCHES

You need to play "Hearts and Flowers" as background music when I tell the story of the watch regulator. My attorney and I tried to sell it to the president of one of the large watch manufacturers and he said, "It's a beautiful idea but we can't use it."

I said, "Why not?", and he said, "Because we advertise a perfect watch and how could we advertise anything better?"

I said, "Well, can't you do what Cadillac does and forget what you said last year and start all over again each year?" He said, "No, we won't."

I said, "Is your watch perfect?" He said, "No, just a good watch, like any other good watch, but we say it's perfect and for most people it's good enough."

"How do you set them?" I asked. He replied, "We always set them a little fast in the factory because no watch can be set correctly. The rate will depend on how you wear it, whether you sleep with it under a blanket or above the blanket, whether you keep the watch on a window or the window open, whether you sleep in a cold or a hot room, whether you are active or sit still all day, and so on. All these things affect a watch." And finally he said, "A fast watch is psychologically all right and a slow watch is psychologically out of order. So, we set them fast and most people don't mind; if they mind, the watch dealer will regulate it for them."

Anyway, I couldn't sell the regulator for nine years, and then I had dinner with an engineer from Chrysler who told me that his boss "hated inaccurate clocks". The boss thought the regulator was a pretty good idea and so the Chrysler people asked the clock industry to incorporate it, and eventually all the other companies fell in line.

So on this invention I did make money—about one hundred and fifty thousand dollars over a period of some ten years. But I did not succeed in selling it to the watch industry. Benrus put it into one of their watches for a while and gave it up because the sales people didn't want to sell it. But, again, customers should never be told that a watch needs regulation. You always tell people that the jeweled watches are perfect. Benrus stopped making watches incorporating my regulator, but I kept a few samples for sentimental reasons.

SELLING IDEAS

This problem of selling inventions is generally far more difficult than the invention itself. The clock regulator is almost an ideal invention in the sense that it makes the clock *better* and at the same time makes it *cheaper*. Still, it took nine years and a lot of disappointments before I could sell the idea. This is true about many of the things I do. But I do them anyway. This is my work and I can think of nothing better to do.

This brings me to the question of incentives. Even if you're crazy like me, you have to have incentives. They are what keeps you trying and you have to try very hard, indeed. Not only do you have to invent, you have to sell the idea—to your own staff, to your superiors, and to many others. Unless you're a dictator, you have to get your own staff enthusiastic about one of your ideas for them to work on it. You've got to sell all the time. In my case I have to sell to my wife and children, and they sometimes are very negative. They have been living with this invention business for a long time and they are not easily impressed. You have to sell to your friends, to your own patent attorney and, of course, you have to sell to the Patent Office, and that's an art in itself. You do sell all the time because you are the kind of guy you are and you have to do it because this is a way of life.

It started when I was very young. I wanted to be an engineer all my life. After graduating from high school, I was talked out of taking an engineering course. I went to the City College of New York and, after a short time, went back to engineering because in 1933 you starved even with a degree. I thought I might just as well starve at something I liked, so I became an engineer. I sold hot dogs at Coney Island, helped to clear snow off the streets of New York, and worked at all sorts of jobs. I worked in factories for ten to twelve dollars per week. Then the National Recovery Administration came in and, as a radio trouble-shooter, I made fourteen dollars per week and my boss complained that he was going to go bankrupt if he had to pay me fourteen dollars a week. It was good experience.

When I tell young engineers how things were then, they seem to think I'm lying, because they can't believe that a man with two degrees could work for twelve to fourteen dollars a week. Even for me, it's hard to remember those days. I learned what it was like to work in a factory and I was surprised that so many people not only don't mind, but actually like routine work. When I was very young I worried as to who was going to do all the dirty and monotonous work in the world. I found that most people don't want to be inventors, or foremen, or leaders. They just like to do a routine job and go home and forget about it. There have been many times, since I've been in business for myself, when I wanted to go home and forget about it too; but for other reasons.

JUST LOVE THEM

How do you fire up students to want to invent? I submit that the most important requirement is teachers who admire inventions. Some time ago I attended a meeting where the speaker, who was wondering how to set up a good laboratory, posed the following question: "If the government wanted to hire, create or discover great artists to create great paintings, how could it build up a stable of people who could create great art? Whom would you appoint as chief and how would he recruit great artists?"

I suggested that the way to do this is like setting up a good laboratory. Get a man who loves art, who understands it, and let him decide. Just give him plenty of funds and tell him to get an organization of artists. If he loves art, he will find his people. If, in addition, he happens to be a good manager and a fine human being, he'll do wonders.

This approach should hold for encouraging inventors. All you have to do to encourage inventors is to love them, to love inventions for their own sake, not necessarily because they make an immediate buck for the corporation. Encourage those things which are emotionally exciting. If you get a man who feels like this, his people will invent.

Very recently I was attending a celebration of the 175th anniversary of the Patent Office's founding, and another speaker remembered my analogizing inventors to women and saying that when the king in Camelot was asked, "How do you make a woman happy?", he replied, "Just love her, love her, nothing else." The speaker continued with his story and said that the trouble with inventors is that it would be nice to "just love them", but that's impossible because "they are such bastards". I don't believe this. We're no more so than any of the rest of the human race. Perhaps we are difficult at times, but then, who isn't?

The way to encourage creativity in school is to get teachers who are better than most of the teachers we have today. This is no exaggeration. High school and undergraduate teachers today, by and large, are terrible, and the reason they're terrible is because their salaries are terrible. My thinking about this is very simple. Double the average salary of the American school teacher and cut his classes in half. This will mean that we will need four times as much money. This will be a lot of money, but it will enable us to hire the kinds of teachers that we need. The government has recently raised the salaries of engineers and it can now get the kinds of engineers it wants. If we have good teachers who love science or love music or love art, the students would love these subjects, too.

We can talk forever about how to increase creativity in school, but unless we get teachers who love creativity, who get fired up, and get a twinkle in their eye when they see a good idea, we're not going to get it from the students. I believe this is true in industry, too. If you have a research director who likes inventions, who respects original work, who can rise above the direct buck-benefit to the company and who can look the other way when a researcher is stealing time to work on something he really likes—and all directors of research, including myself, do this—then you have the kind of boss whose people will invent. And if you have the other kind of boss who doesn't like inventions, for whatever reason, you're not going to get inventions, because people are very practical. They will not beat their brains out for somebody who doesn't want them to do original thinking.

I've heard teachers complain that students don't ask enough interesting questions. I suspect that the trouble is that by the time a bright kid gets to college, he knows that most teachers are afraid of difficult questions, so he gets wise and doesn't ask them. The young children in kindergarten don't know this yet. Also, the questions they can ask are probably answerable by the teacher.

In industry, people who say that they would like to have very active inventors, would like to encourage them, and to pursue their ideas in any area, really don't mean this. Most managers in industry want inventors who invent in a very narrow field. In other words, most managers want an inventor who will solve their problems, not his problems. This is typical and normal. They want an inventor who is specialized in their business and doesn't invent anything else. Harry Diamond, who at one time was my boss, and after whom the ordnance laboratory in Washington is now named, used to say —I'll clean up his statement a little bit—"Everybody wants a southern Negro from as far North as possible."

In summary, what I want to say about the difficulty an inventor faces is this: Nobody wants his inventions. They want his brains. He can get a good salary, but you can't interest people in his really original inventions. The way to improve that, perhaps, is to get industry leaders and heads of laboratories to really want inventions for their own sake.

I was once talking about this to Sherman Fairchild, who is both an inventor and a very successful businessman, and what he said was, "You know, Jack, the trouble is that inventions aren't worth a damn, but inventors are very valuable people!"

DISCUSSION
Inventing Within Relevant Missions

JACK MORTON: Could an inventor increase the probability of invention— loading the dice one might say—by knowing what business he is in and, therefore, being better able to identify the sources of information he needs? For example, like a miner who knows where to look for gold.

JACOB RABINOW: When one narrows his specialization, he probably comes up with fewer ideas. If one loads the dice in favor of a certain art, one cuts off analogous arts, which I think are important. The more an inventor can pull out of related *and* unrelated arts, the more original his ideas are likely to be.

JACK MORTON: You mentioned the very difficult problem of not only selling the invention, but also finding the capital to support its development. If an invention is therefore to be part of a modern business, it must be relevant, I should think, to the goals of that business.

JACOB RABINOW: You are talking about the needs of the entrepreneur or the manager, and there is no question that he cannot blindly support research, no matter how beautiful it is, in fields which have no relevance to his enterprise. But the question I am addressing myself to is, how do we bring out inventiveness in individuals, and I feel that we should encourage them if at all possible. I have asked people at Bell Laboratories what they do when an employee invents something which is not remotely connected with telephones—like a cure for cancer. The answer was, "We'd support it." I said, "That's very nice, but what would you do if he did something not quite so spectacular?" And the answer was, "We would probably give him a little money, or give him some time to work on it, but not encourage it too much." But, you see, even a little bit of encouragement shows you care.

EMANUEL PIORE: I'm inclined to agree with Jack Rabinow regarding the need to give some encouragement to inventors, even when their activities are irrelevant. We had an employee in one of our labs whose child died of leukemia. He wanted to do something about this problem and got involved in the development of blood separators, offering his assistance to the National Institutes of Health. Well, the local management gave him time off, but wouldn't even pay his travel expenses to Washington—until the upper management heard about it and raised hell with the local people. This illustrates some of the difficulty that top management has in the area of encouraging its employees. The problem is how to get the word down below. This is a very basic problem.

Employee Rights in Inventions

CALVIN TAYLOR: I hear from some inventors that we need to straighten out the incentive system in industry before we move back into the schools to encourage creativity. They say that by and large, inventors have to sign away all of their rights in their future inventions before they can get a job in a corporation.

JACOB RABINOW: There are other kinds of incentives, such as salary increases, prestigious titles, fringe benefits, elegant laboratories and equipment, and they are, I think, reward enough. I don't think the patent rights make much difference.

The Randomness of Invention

ROBERT DEAN: If it is felt that invention is a random process, does this mean that systematic logic has no role in the development of new ideas?

JACOB RABINOW: No, there are many problems you attack logically. In life, in economics, in technology, there are many problems for which the logical approach works beautifully, because you don't have to invent. If you come to me and ask, "How do you stabilize an oscillating car on the road?", I can tell you logically how to take the oscillation problem and lick it by proper damping. If you ask me how to guide an airplane or a missile, I can give you logical approaches. There's nothing wrong with a pure, straight, logical approach, but this is not invention.

There *is* a logical sequence associated with invention and that is to check to see if the conception is good. You get a crazy idea, and then you start going logically through the ABC's of physics or chemistry and find that the idea will or will not work. Good inventors do this first, before their enemies do it, which is one of the things that distinguishes the crackpot from the inventor.

EMANUEL PIORE: Conant wrote a book on science using case histories.* He took some case histories in chemistry, of people who were very creative chemists. The book shows that for all the ballyhooing about the scientific method, no creative scientist uses it. This is one of the problems that some

---

* James Bryant Conant (ed.), *Harvard Case Histories in Experimental Science*. Harvard University Press, Cambridge: 1957.

DISCUSSION

of the operational researchers, who look over the shoulders of engineers and scientists, would like to structure.

JACOB RABINOW: At the end of World War II we had a great many engineers and scientists, in our laboratory at the National Bureau of Standards, with lots of time. One of the things we did with our time was to analyze proximity fuses logically: What kinds of targets were there, what kinds of forces were available to "feel" the target, and so on. (A proximity fuse is a device that "feels" the target at a distance.) We took the whole range of factors and possibilities and analyzed them exhaustively. In the matrix of boxes we would place a plus if the possibility was realistic and zero if it could not be done. This was a logical, methodical approach aimed at covering the whole spectrum of energy, versus targets, versus sources. There was one box which was zero, because it was logically impossible. I invented a fuse that used that possibility very effectively, though I can't tell you about it because it's still classified.

L. M. BOELTER: You said that teachers are needed in our schools who have a fondness and respect for creativity. Did you mean all kinds of teachers, or only teachers in the technical fields?

JACOB RABINOW: All kinds of teachers—in poetry, in English, in languages, in writing, in art, in the sciences, in anything where originality is important.

CHAPTER 7

INNOVATION AND ENTREPRENEURSHIP

RICHARD S. MORSE

INNOVATION is a basic characteristic of American society and has been an essential factor contributing to the phenomenal growth of this country. There are many elements of the innovative process, including science, technology, engineering, production management, marketing, finance and many other operations which, in the aggregate, contribute to the introduction of new and useful products, processes and services into the economy.

THE ENTREPRENEUR

Throughout the innovative process one finds an entrepreneur who, either alone or as an inspirer and leader of a group effort, combats the conservative nature of man and drives forward with new untried ideas until they are finally introduced in the market place. An entrepreneur encompasses more than the functions of an inventor, a project manager, a salesman or a financier. Entrepreneurs exist in both large and small corporations. Some industries cultivate the entrepreneurial spirit; others have characteristics which impede entrepreneurial activities. The ability to develop a conducive environment for entrepreneurship is of major interest to progressive and innovative-minded managers in many large American corporations. They are experimenting with new approaches to enhance the success of entrepreneurial efforts, both within their corporate structure and through the medium of external mechanisms for profitable growth—for example, joint ventures with small innovative companies and organizational changes to enhance innovation.

TECHNOLOGY TRANSFER

In recent years we have read much about the technology transfer process: the ability to convert processes, products or technology from space and defense activities into useful applications in the civilian sector of the business world. Many approaches are being tried to facilitate this technology transfer process, but we should not forget that, fundamentally, this is not a problem of information transfer or the dissemination of technical data. Technology transfer is basically a "people transfer" process. It is people who take ideas and do things with them. An effective entrepreneur, who has the ability to exploit commercial applications of science and technology, is far more useful to a profit-oriented corporation than many millions spent upon research and development, which for lack of entrepreneurial skill, bad timing, or lack of market acceptance, may never result in salable, profitable products.

There are many misconceptions regarding the role of basic research and the ability to generate consumer or industrial products as a direct result of our military and space R & D activities. Basic research and advanced development constitute essential building blocks for subsequent new technologies in the innovation process. Relatively few people have the competence to perform basic research, and this field is now clearly "people limited" in the sense that more funds are now available for basic research than can be applied to really first-class scientific talent.

It is the application of technology, perhaps some years down the road from prior basic research in any field, which is of primary importance in terms of tangible benefits to man. Occasionally, a useful new product may be evolved directly from our military aerospace programs, but neither the spending of dollars nor the writing of voluminous reports, *per se,* serves a persuasive function in terms of economic growth or the creation of jobs.

In all cases, dedicated and enthusiastic people with entrepreneurial talents are essential to take new ideas, processes, product concepts or technologies, and convert them into useful things for which there is a demand in the market place. The United States has a remarkable capacity for generating new enterprises, and one of the most interesting features of economic growth, in the areas of science and technology particularly, is the rate at which new ventures are launched in this country through the efforts of entrepreneurs who see opportunities for forming corporations and rapidly entering the market place with new services and products.

INCREASING REQUIREMENTS FOR ENTRY AND SURVIVAL

Various ingredients go into the innovative process, and in our highly competitive industrial society, each of these plays an important role. The problems associated with the development of a new business enterprise, or the launching of a new product, are far more complicated than is commonly appreciated—and more so now than in the past. New technology is being generated at a very high rate, marketing problems are extensive and complex, and the higher mobility of people puts great emphasis upon the timing of any new product or business enterprise.

The critical size for the survival of a new company is larger than ever because of the cost of doing business today. Initial capital requirements are perhaps ten times higher today than in 1940. Research is far more complex and expensive, and the lack of stability and sense of business reality of many scientists and engineers, many of whom are literally "in space", presents real problems to new ventures and to the men themselves.

While it appears that this country has more than adequate supplies of potentially available venture capital, the venture capital business itself is not well understood. If a small fraction of 1 per cent of the capital available from progressive insurance companies, large corporations, successful entrepreneurs, individual millionaires, investment funds, and small business investment companies were devoted to the funding of new enterprises, quantities of venture capital would certainly be available far in excess of worthwhile endeavours that might be found. The supply of venture capital, and the use of organized mechanisms for its investment, is, however, relatively unknown in many parts of the country. While an abundance of venture capital is potentially available in the United States, this in itself is no assurance that an entrepreneur will either find it available for his program or even know how to present his case to a receptive source of money.

PROJECT APPRAISAL

From the viewpoint of the capital source, the problem of project appraisal is indeed a formidable one. Financial institutions, and the people associated with them, are normally not experienced in the field of new enterprises and the management problems associated with their generation. There is a great need for a better understanding of the entrepreneur–capital relationship and mechanisms must be developed to enhance the ability of entrepreneurs and capital sources to communicate with one another. Techniques must also be evolved for capital sources to perform more effectively the appraisal function of people, ideas, markets and technologies, in order to reduce potential risks which are always associated with both the generation of new enterprises and the financing of innovative ideas.

Experience suggests that innovative operations fail, first of all, because of a misjudgment of markets. The entrepreneur by nature is an optimistic enthusiast, and too early an entry into the market place with a product can be just as disastrous as being too late. Not only must there be a ready customer acceptance for the entrepreneur's new product, but, in addition, problems of cost and marketing become increasingly important, particularly for later products when competition has also become a critical factor. Really successful products reach the market at the right time and at the right price, a task which indeed calls for uncommon management abilities or, in some cases, just good luck—a factor which is difficult either to evaluate or predict.

BENEFICIAL ENVIRONMENTS

It appears that certain environments are conducive to the entrepreneurial spirit, and that this is a subject which is not completely understood. It deserves further study. It has been suggested that the ingredients essential to the generation of new enterprises often include graduate schools, government research laboratories, and venturesome capital sources. While this may well be true, it would appear that these ingredients alone are not enough.

There are many sections of the country, for example, which have an abundance of technical talent and good universities, and yet essentially no new entrepreneurial activities have taken place. Philadelphia and Chicago, for example, might well be included in this category. Some of the other major cities have an abundance of wealthy individuals who would welcome opportunities to participate in the generation of new enterprises, but no mechanism is available for marshalling their capital or talents, nor have techniques been evolved for ferreting out the latent entrepreneurial skills which no doubt are present in every section of the United States. In contrast, the Great Boston and Palo Alto areas are often cited as prime examples of successful new enterprise generation. Both regions have, in fact, engendered an environment conducive to entrepreneurial activities.

In short, one might say that entrepreneurship breeds entrepreneurship. If one establishes a precedent of successful new enterprise generation and, in addition, ideas, venture capital, technology, and graduate schools are present in a region, the system seems to get under way probably because of the initial stimulus of one or more exemplary individuals in the area.

The entrepreneurial spirit can make a substantial contribution to economic growth, industrial diversification, and the development of a city, region, or country. A recent analysis of some 21 new technically based companies in the Boston area showed an increase in sales of $76,000,000 over a period of about four years. During this same period some 3000 jobs were provided. The average amount of *initial* venture capital required to establish these 21 companies was $225,000 per company. Expressed in another manner, new jobs were created in the area at a cost per job of $1525 of initial venture capital investment.

While the environment is particularly important in any given region if the innovative process is to flourish, this is likewise true in both industries and corporations. Effective innovative operations and entrepreneurship are always dependent upon people, but the character of certain industries and companies is often such that the latent talents of the inventor or entrepreneur lie dormant, and the company's ability to attract entrepreneurial skills may be totally lacking. In our current and rapidly changing technological environment, we are seeing major changes in the growth as well as profitability of both industrial groups and corporate entities within such groups. A better knowledge of innovation and its problems, particularly at the management level, must be recognized by all progressive executives. Innovative individuals and entrepreneurs are dedicated to the concept of change, an objective also in keeping with modern management attitudes. Opportunities for growth at the corporate level today usually arise outside the company's current historical product line and this places an increased burden upon management to utilize innovative techniques throughout the corporate operation.

Bearing in mind that it is always *people* who innovate and serve as our source of entrepreneurial talent, we should have concern for the future in view of the relatively large numbers of skilled professional scientists and engineers who are wholly committed to federally funded R & D programs in defense and space. We are currently restricting a large segment of our technical and professional manpower to areas of activity which preclude their ever developing the experience so essential to the introduction of innovative ideas into the civilian sector of the economy. A long and continued association with government contracts and programs has removed a large percentage of potential technical managers and entrepreneurs from our society, in the sense that they may permanently lose their ability to develop new processes or products which are capable of being economically developed, manufactured and introduced into the market place.

GREATER UNDERSTANDING NEEDED

We are indeed fortunate in this country that we have developed such a fine working relationship between government, industry and our universities. This arrangement, bred in wartime, represents a major factor in our attempts to solve many national problems. In the field of innovation, and the development of a better understanding of the process, all three of these segments of society have an important role to play. Government, from the viewpoint of regulation, taxation and R & D funding, has much to learn. At various levels within our government agencies and departments, better appreciation of the innovative process and its significant contribution to economic growth must be developed. Progressive industrial managers are already concerned about the problems of innovation and are experimenting with new concepts of entrepreneurship. A far larger percentage of these managers, to say nothing of those in the less progressive industries, must recognize the role of innovation and invention and make such changes in both management and organizational structures as appear indicated.

Further information must be developed about the innovative

process through research, and this can quite logically be undertaken in our graduate schools of management, in collaboration with government and industry. The process is not fully understood and many misconceptions are prevalent. Much "research on research" needs to be done.

The more progressive companies are usually the first to recognize the needs for studying entrepreneurship in order to examine new mechanisms whereby the innovative process can be employed more effectively within the corporation or undertaken in collaboration with new technical enterprises. For example, several of the large corporations are, in a sense, serving as sources of venture capital and experimenting with new and innovative procedures, whereby they can work with new technically based ventures on a mutually profitable basis. As might be expected, new concepts of this type are coming from companies that have already been successful in adapting the innovative process to their corporate goals. They do not, as a rule, come from the older and less progressive segments of industry. Yet these segments have greater need for the application of technology and innovative management techniques to solve their current and future operating problems and to develop a corporate image which will attract the types of people interested in creative activity.

Interesting mechanisms are currently being evolved by some large corporations which permit closer collaboration with small innovative companies. This represents a new and novel approach to combining the high level of entrepreneurial skills found in small technical ventures with the availability of capital, marketing experience and management talent found in large corporations. The most successful procedures to be employed for such intercorporate relations are still in a state of evolution, but continued studies based on experience in this field should prove very interesting and instructive. These relations may well offer one of the most successful methods for the exploitation of advanced technology and the skills of the inventor and entrepreneur.

Little information is currently available regarding the impact of new innovative operations on the economy as a whole. There is an abundance of evidence to demonstrate that many of the really new ideas come from individuals and small companies not directly involved with large corporate structures. We must know more about the characteristics of the entrepreneur and inventor and make an effort to cultivate an appropriate environment within our educational system and society as a whole, so that we can enhance the effectiveness of innovation and reap the appropriate rewards both within this country and throughout the world.

REWARDS FOR WINNERS

Rewards are, of course, of importance to both the entrepreneur, his key people, and venture capital sources, whether these be corporate or individual. But technological innovation is a tortuous process requiring new ideas in management, finance and sales, as well as in advanced technology.

Fortunately, this country does offer personal and financial incentives to both individuals and corporations. New companies are being generated at an increasing rate, and in spite of the fact that we do have substantial taxes, some 5000 millionaires per year are added to American society. In one segment of the Boston area alone, the *personal* net worth of the "Route 128" entrepreneurs now far exceeds $500,000,000. The road to success is difficult, but never before has any country offered opportunities, like those in the U.S., for an innovative individual to have fun, make money, and leave a lasting imprint on his country and local community.

DISCUSSION

Small-company Problems

JACOB RABINOW: I am convinced that the possibilities of a small company succeeding have changed for the worse in the last several years. After the war, it was relatively easy to start a company and be successful, because the large corporations were up to their necks in their ongoing markets. In the last four or five years, as the large corporations have increased their markets, the smaller companies have begun to fail more rapidly. Why? Before, the larger companies didn't care about smaller, diversified markets. Now that they have saturated their traditional markets, they are turning to the smaller markets and it is very difficult for small companies to compete with large corporations that can put out the large effort needed to enlarge their businesses. Patents cannot save a small company unless it has a very basic invention, of which there are so few they are memorable. It is much more difficult for an entrepreneur to form a successful small company now than it was ten years ago.

RICHARD MORSE: I agree that the small-company problems today are more difficult than they were 10 or 20 years ago. Because of the complexity and costs of R & D, larger technical staffs are required and higher investments are necessary for research facilities. The amount of venture capital

DISCUSSION

required for a new technical enterprise is now much larger than was the case 10 years ago, and problems of marketing are particularly difficult for a firm having less than $2 or $5 million in sales per year.

Nevertheless, small companies tend to have and retain a spirit of entrepreneurship, drive and innovative thinking that is not often present in large corporations. They can move faster and get into a market place sooner, particularly with new and specialized products and processes. I am convinced that opportunity still exists for the small company. Even though the game is different, the challenge is still there and the current records of many successful entrepreneurs today are by no means discouraging.

Second Generation Products

C. D. W. THORNTON: The basic problem, though, is that of the second generation product. In my company we often see one of our divisions challenged by outside companies that have introduced the next generation product on the market, even though they were not first in the business. Those of us engaged in "finding" companies for acquisition know that we have to pay a good deal of attention to whether there is going to be a second generation set of products from the company being considered. The cost of developing a second generation product is a lot higher than that of the first generation effort.

JACOB RABINOW: There is a special problem which the small entrepreneur faces which isn't often recognized and which, I think, has been aggravated in the last five years. It is now more important than ever before to have good legal, accounting, and technical advice. The large company can afford to have a large number of attorneys, and a large number of various experts, from whom they can get good advice. The small entrepreneur has to hire these one at a time. It is much more difficult, takes much more research time, and requires proportionately greater expenditures.

When I was president of Rabinow Electronics, I had, on my board of directors, a senior partner from a good Wall Street firm, a research director of Gillette, a division manager of Cutler–Hammer, a very good lawyer, and an outstanding patent attorney. In spite of all this advice (and I listened—I'm conceited in inventions, but not in business) we still didn't make a go of it in that second generation of products. This is generally true of small companies. Even if the small company wins the first race, the large company will win in the long run.

I have worked as a consultant for some large companies. The president of one of them said to me once: "You know, it doesn't make any difference who comes out with a new product. Once the market's established, unless there is some really peculiar circumstance, we'll have the product on sale a year later and have 60 per cent of the sales, no matter who started it." And this is also true of computers. I respect IBM very much; it's a very large company and it does an excellent job. No matter what some inventor may do in computers, two years later IBM will still have 70–75 per cent of the market.

This is not because of any difference in the cost of second generation products. I think the difficulty is that small companies do not have the sustaining power that many large corporations have. The day when the big corporations compete with us (the small companies) in our own markets is the day we perish, and this is something the government should be worried about.

DISCUSSION

The future is very small for the independent inventor, but it's very beautiful for an employee-inventor. Inventors, by and large, can do very well in large companies.

Changing Social Patterns

DONALD SCHON: I wonder if you could distinguish between the problem of innovation and the development of new small companies based on a new technology and the problem of entrepreneurship and innovation in a large established firm? How many of these large companies have experienced the problem of where the next dollar is going to come from in as acute a form as the small ones do? I wonder if Mr. Morse would care to throw some light on the kind of teaching, or the kind of insights taught, regarding the entrepreneurial process in these two different places. It seems to me, for example, that we're experiencing a change in social patterns. The last 50 years have seen the flowering of lots of little companies based on inventions, but now we see companies like IBM and 3M, where the large company begins to serve as an umbrella over the formation of new small businesses from within, completely changing the characteristics of the entrepreneurial pattern.

Government Contracting

RICHARD MORSE: The climate for entrepreneurship and innovation has changed. The impact of federal activities on both the small and large innovative corporation *is* very important today. We are all familiar with small companies that must face technical or market risks which may be so large that *one* mistake can destroy the company. A big company like General Electric, however, can bury its mistakes under other government contracts, or aspects of the business, so that even multimillion dollar bad risks, or errors in R & D, or product development programs, are of minor importance on the over-all business of the company. Some government policies militate against the success of the small company. They should be changed. We have this cost-sharing idea in R & D, for example, where a large corporation will undercut the bidding and say, "Well, I've got a half-million of my own money and will 'cost share' this program to buy into the business."

I think the small company has problems in that it now needs a more rounded management team even to get started in today's environment. Venture capital sources, for example, are usually looking not only for a new growth product or process, but a complete management team. They know that you need more than just one or two things in your favor to be successful. They realize that first or second generation products are not enough. A recent national survey of various sources of venture capital indicated primary interest from the investor viewpoint in growth prospects for the product and the quality of the management group. In general, the small company has to have a really sophisticated technology so that it at least has a technical jump on the large company.

The problem of entrepreneurship in the large firm is currently being studied by many of the more progressive corporations. The more successful experiments suggest using organizational structures that permit the innovative individual or entrepreneur in a large company to have maximum flexibility and responsibility for the exploitation of his complete program— research, development, engineering, marketing, and so on. This may mean permitting the man with drive and ability at the lower level to have access to higher authority and the use of corporate facilities outside his normal channels as defined by usual organizational boundaries.

Many companies are, of course, now looking outside their organizations for entrepreneurship, particularly in technical areas removed from their normal field of competence. We see large companies entering the venture capital business, forming joint ventures, or funding research with other companies in order to expand more rapidly in technical fields which offer growth prospects.

Bigness is Relative

JACK MORTON: I would like to pull a few of these ideas together and then make a comment about bigness versus smallness. At least, I hope that this group is not convinced that bigness in itself is bad. The size of a corporation, or the size of an organization, is always to be measured against the size of the job. Bigness is relative and only that. In our discussions I detect a consensus that creativity is a necessary ingredient in innovation, and I think most of us would agree that innovation is a process and not a single act. Creativity is involved in research, discovery of new knowledge, in its application, in developmental engineering, in the manufacture of the hardware involved, in marketing and sales, in the raising of capital, and in the supplying of services.

One of the reasons why small companies have difficulty is that eventually they try to reach the market place. They are trying to innovate in an economic sense, and if the innovative process is a series of connected steps as I have mentioned, the small company is very apt to be strong in only one of the parts of the innovative process, and not in all of them. In order to be effective over a span of time you must either be effective in all steps of the innovative process, or you must get yourself tied in with an outfit which is strong in all the steps. One of the reasons why IBM has been so successful is because they are effective in all steps of the innovative process, including service. It isn't just because they are big.

ROBERT CHARPIE: We tend to lose sight of the central figure in the innovative process. He is the entrepreneur.

It is very important not to get hung-up on distinctions in corporate size, but to focus on the creative act itself. When we do that, we come back to the realization that the entrepreneurial act is fundamentally different from the experience gained in our traditional education. The competent technical man in industry has additional boundary conditions on his actions, including the necessity to make a profit and to operate in the market place, testing his mettle against different competitors of different sizes, with different capabilities.

My concern has been how to bring into engineering education the kind of mettle-testing which we see in the business world, which somehow has to be brought in as an additional boundary condition, if we are to create people who have good technical competence and can also manage and steer an enterprise, however big it may be or whatever form it may assume, so that their technical ideas and technical skills can finally appear as an innovative contribution to society. I don't see that these considerations about size are anything but collateral.

DISCUSSION

Learning to Swim

C. STARK DRAPER: The people who work in our Instrumentation Laboratory at M.I.T. are exposed to the idea that they are in an arena where there is no justice, nobody they can depend upon for fair play, and where they've got to watch out that their backsides are not damaged by somebody they thought was a friend. You must have people in contact with realities. It is essential that they realize what the circumstances are going to be, and we try very hard to have them come in contact with this experience. As far as knowing who can do this and who can't, I don't know how you can find out if a guy can swim unless you throw him in the water.

CHAPTER 8

TRADE-OFFS AND CONSTRAINTS

ROBERT C. DEAN, JR.

DEVELOPING creative education is a social problem; it is not really a technical problem at all. Nevertheless, anyone who tries to structure an effect or outcome behaves like an engineer. In the common parlance, we talk about "engineering a victory" in war, or "engineering a victory" in a political campaign. I think we have the same sort of a problem here. The science involved may be very weak, and I'm sure it is, but still there is some knowledge and we must draw upon it.

The engineer sets out to solve a human need with all the tools and the craft that he can command, and I think that's exactly what we should be trying to do with respect to engineering education.

First, it is necessary to recognize the problem by identifying the human need. The need is to obtain a significantly higher level of practical exploitation of the inherent creative talents of engineers. The task before us is to make an improvement in engineering creativity using the educational system in cooperation with many other social systems, such as industry, government, and professional societies. We are attempting to use the educational system to improve our ability to bring forth man's inherent creativity.

The next thing we must do is to examine the constraints that will bind any acceptable solution. When we first start out, there are always too many constraints. We raise many ghosts, which we have to demolish. One of the characteristics of a good inventor is that he has learned not to accept many of the constraints that other people feel are fundamental. We must pare back this problem to its essentials. I shall try to make a tentative listing now of the constraints on the development of creative engineering education, as I see them.

First, any solution that we devise must be appropriate to the social value it may generate, now and in the future. It is very easy to say that if one wants a maximum amount of creativity from education, there should be a maximum effort applied to its generation. But in the business of education, we have a very serious problem. That is, if we try too hard, we may end up with a negative result, as we did when we placed such great emphasis on bringing more science into engineering. The pendulum has swung, many of us feel, much too far toward scientific training of engineers, and in the process we have harmed engineering education.

The key problem is a proper balance between discipline and imagination. Too much science is too much discipline; too much imagination is too little science. Anyone who tries to teach the practice of creative engineering, or entrepreneurship, or whatever we wish to call it, is always faced with the problem of making a proper balance between discipline and imagination.

If we push too hard in developing creative engineering education, eventually the pendulum will swing the other way—back toward science. We could easily produce such a negative reaction. As we approach this ticklish problem, therefore, we must be very careful to avoid fads. "Creativity" and "design" are two catchwords that are now running heavily through the field of engineering education.

I was amazed, when we sought applicants for a workshop in engineering education at Dartmouth, over the great penetration that the word "design" has made into engineering education, even to the extent that many schools seem to be convinced that they should base all the undergraduate education on the word "design". They look around their faculty to see who can teach design. The only people they can find are the graphics teachers. So, believe it or not, in many schools the graphics teachers are becoming the principal leaders of the development of new educational methods. And I personally feel that they are probably the least able to lead the development of the engineering for the future that Dr. Hollomon has sketched.

The second constraint on any solution we might generate is that any short-term plans we might present must be used by present-day teachers. When I examine faculties and schools, I find that faculties are very frequently conservative. They are afraid of experimentation; they are afraid of entrepreneurship in education. That is probably one reason why they are teachers, because they have left behind them some aspects of the real world and retired into a somewhat artificial world. Our task, therefore, is to produce something that this sort of man will try and will adopt.

In the long term, in changing engineering education, we probably will have to make a significant alteration in the nature of the teachers. There are many difficulties in the doing of this. I am not even sure that a major change can be made, although there have been changes in some special instances. But I am sure that, if we want to engender a fundamental advance in education for creativity, we must have a different sort of teacher. At least some teachers, maybe twenty per cent of the faculty in an engineering school, will have to be very different from the teacher of today. But even these different sorts of people are still people; we must recognize that this is very much a human problem.

The next constraint that we must heed is that the cost of any solution we propose must not exceed our *cash* resources. I underline the word *cash* because, no matter what the ultimate value of this may be to society, there is only so much money available. We can say that vast amounts of money perhaps should be available for this critical task, but that is just dreaming. There is only so much money available at any time. In the future, however, we can change the availability of cash, if we have demonstrated results showing that what we are doing "makes a buck" for society, so to speak.

There is a very severe criticism which can be aimed at us educators—and I am surprised it's not aimed more often—namely, why teach engineering practice, or the practice of creative engineering in school? Why not teach it in industry, where the real situations exist? Many of us have been saying that the way to teach creativity is to put students in real situations. Or, as Stark Draper has put it, if you want to see whether a man can swim or not, throw him in the water. There is no better way to throw a man into the water than to put him in industry. So why should we make the student swim in school? This is a serious question which demands a serious answer.

The fourth constraint is that any solution we propose to this problem must be self-justifying. It must have built into it means for testing its success. All of us who are educational entrepreneurs are continually worried about *how* we test our success, and test on a rather short-term basis. We must test to prove our value to society. We must test because the way we start out may be the wrong way and we must therefore change our strategies with experience. So we must have a feedback of information, and how we will get this I do not know. I do not think anybody knows how to measure the success of education unless he has been in the business for thirty years, like Stark Draper, who has had twenty-seven companies spun off his activity, and a hundred and thirty students who hold important positions. But thirty years is perhaps too long a time to wait.

We need a very hard-nosed approach to this problem. We must not just pick solutions that look good on paper, or sound good when presented. We must pick a course that will ultimately stand the test of time.

The fifth constraint is that the solution to this problem must be self-regenerating. I think we would all agree that the exploitation of creativity is a continuing social need. Man has always needed to use his creative abilities better. I do not think we are going to solve this problem in the next hundred years. Therefore, anything we do now to improve engineering education must continue; it must not be a flash in the pan. And we must realize that we are shooting at a moving target because, as man's potential to creatively express himself increases, I'm sure that we will want more. The capabilities exposed and the new challenges that will arise will demand still greater talents and results. As good inventors, I think, we will look at what we have done, and probably feel it is not very good, because we will feel a power to do very much better. Human needs are so vast that we shall never in our lifetime, or our children's, see a gain that we can be complacent over.

The sixth constraint that I suggest is obvious, but not easy to achieve. The solution we propose must be realistic, and it must be realistic with regard to all the manifold influences of the environment that affects our students. We have all heard about the early education of students at home and in the early school years, and how this affects what they do in college. The psychologists are very much concerned about this.

We must consider society's ethics and value systems, for it is well recognized that society both encourages and dampens creative endeavors. We must examine lower-school teaching to see if there is anything that can be done there to improve the situation in the engineering school. Career opportunities demand careful study. For example, we are trying at Dartmouth to educate technological entrepreneurs. Whenever we say that to engineering educators, they advise that we are educating engineers that nobody will want. Our graduates are predicted to be a drag on the market because they will be revolutionaries, hard to get along with, and unwanted in conventional industry. We are accused of turning out men who will only go off and start their own shops. We do not accept these criticisms because we believe that the job of the engineer is to change the world, and that one of the most important places to produce change is in the big company. But this conviction must be proved; perhaps nobody will want our graduates and we will have to change our *modus operandi*. The entire matter is very important. What is the market for engineers? What sort of man should one put into the market place? If we graduate a man who is way ahead of his time, perhaps he may not carry out the task that we intended for him.

There are still other educational requirements, which bring us back to discipline versus imagination. The educator is obliged to transmit the knowledge and facts that have been generated by past generations and to give it to our young people to use. For instance, the inventor depends very much upon his factual knowledge. In contrast, there is a great tendency in teaching creativity to ignore facts, and to emphasize the student's imagination. But this, I feel, is a very dangerous thing to do.

We also need to examine the students' capabilities, the psychological factors that inhibit him, and how these can be changed, if at all. One good example, which can be very dismaying, is in attempting to educate foreign students to be entrepreneurs. I once had a Nigerian, a Jordanian, and a Korean in a class called "Internship in Engineering". I found that these foreigners drowned when we "threw them into the water". They weren't prepared to even try to swim, and we drowned a number of them.

These are a few of the constraints on the task of improving engineering education for creativity. I want to emphasize again that the education of teachers comes first. A commendable experiment was carried out in the summer of 1965, and I was very fortunate to have been a part of it. The experiment had been proposed by the Commission on Engineering Education and it was generously supported by the National Science Foundation.

The proposal was that a system of workshops be set up across the nation, which would educate teachers to teach design. Six workshops were conducted at six different colleges across the country. Some twenty-eight teachers were passed through the various workshops. If the experiment did nothing else, it stimulated the participants by bringing them into contact with men in certain schools who have been educational entrepreneurs, trying to introduce new ideas. Each workshop involved about six faculty members, who each brought with them four of their own students to teach. Instructing their own students was a device to counter the psychological defense often made by a visiting teacher: "Well, you can do that with students at your university, but not with mine." So they were asked to bring their own students.

The workshops' objectives were to stimulate design teachers, coach them in methodology, and acquaint them with the problems. They were aided in devising courses in creative engineering at their own schools.

There were twenty-four applicants for the six positions in the Dartmouth Workshop. We examined these teachers' credentials very carefully. They wrote essays about why they should come and what they were going to do with the experience. Their deans indicated what each would do to support his man when he came back to his school.

We were very surprised to find that not one of these twenty-four teachers of design (and they were a select group) had any significant engineering experience. They had never held a financially responsible position in engineering where they had to meet deadlines and payrolls. This was a pretty large sample of design teachers, and yet not one of them had ever had any real engineering experience.

The first act was to subject the teachers to a realistic engineering project. This was a new experience for them all. I was chief engineer and one of my colleagues who has had a fair amount of engineering experience was my assistant. We picked the problem of weighing hospital patients in bed. This turns out to be a fairly serious, practical problem, for it is difficult to move the severely injured out of bed on to conventional weighing devices.

The first step was to recognize the need; that is, to find the problem. We visited hospitals and talked to their staffs. Next we prepared and, later on, operated a plan for the project. This was the first experience of any one of these teachers in planning a project. Some of them were department heads, and some were assistant deans. I was amazed to find that in administrative and academic affairs, an engineering approach to problems apparently is just not adopted.

We struggled with the economics of both the solution and the project. We made market studies. The project had constraints, including time schedules and a money budget. We lost money. We contacted some fifty potential users making, I believe, a fairly good market study over the telephone. The teacher-staff invented many alternatives, evaluated them, and finally boiled them down to two. These were evaluated as well as possible in the time available, and a report was written and presented. I think the workshop faculty did very well, although not without much misgiving and many internal struggles and frustration. We had a couple of faculty members who just would not give up their pet ideas, despite the fact that they could not challenge the decision systems that had been set up, and they could not introduce any new data which would indicate that the decisions were wrong.

These teachers actually solved a real problem and came up with a good solution for weighing patients in bed. They were proud of this fact, but they were frustrated, because they were not sure that their device would ever be put into practice. The same problem is experienced with respect to student inventions.

The workshop faculty also taught our sophomore course "Introduction to Engineering". It is a course in engineering practice in which the sophomores, who have not yet been "spoiled", are given a real engineering problem. In this particular workshop the students were required to design mobility aids for the crippled. The students set up budgets and carried out all the phases of an engineer's job. The students amazed the faculty with what they could do.

The students struggled with the economics of the problem, the market for the device, the trials of reduction to practice, and the risks involved in entrepreneurship. Of course, the students did none of these things with any great expertise, but they did try very hard, and their solutions were not too bad. Out of six student "companies", three produced important new developments in the field of rehabilitation. At least the results were so judged by manufacturers, chief engineers, and by rehabilitation and medical experts.

One of the devices was a rather remarkable device called the "Upalator". It was designed and built in eight weeks by four students. It actually worked and was praised by the rehabilitation and engineering evaluators. In fact, the students were encouraged to patent certain aspects.

Three of the student "companies" worked on curb-climbing wheelchairs. Surprisingly, one of the worst problems that they encountered in mobility for the cripples is getting over a simple curb, ranging from two to eight inches in height. The three groups tackled this problem. The most promising solution was extremely simple. A manufacturer of wheelchairs discussed buying the design after he saw it demonstrated, and this was most encouraging to the students, for they felt that they had done something useful and wanted to see it used.

This raises a very serious problem, particularly from two aspects. Our students do this sort of thing all the time. They carry devices to this stage, where they have proved to be useful. But what do they do with it from that point? They are naturally frustrated if nothing further happens. If we had some means for carrying on the reduction to practice of these student-developed devices, I think it would greatly aid creative engineering education.

We have briefly explored two aspects of education for creativity. First, a means to educate teachers and, second, a means to educate students to be creative. Students can be highly creative, and at Dartmouth we are very pleased with the results of this sort of education. But the particular approach we use is certainly not the only one. Moreover, it may be suitable only to a place like Dartmouth where we have a relatively small number of engineering students. Many engineering schools have vastly larger student bodies and different kinds of problems. Consequently, different approaches may be preferable at other schools.

PART 3

THE OPPORTUNITIES

CHAPTER 9

EDUCATIONAL OBJECTIVES IN THE PREPARATION OF ENGINEERS*

B. RICHARD TEARE, JR.

IN THE last decade or so there has been an increasing emphasis on applied science and mathematics in both undergraduate and graduate engineering work. Courses that might develop creativeness have been squeezed out of curricula in favor of others which cover new subject matter. New recruits to the teaching profession have been found among graduates who have just received their doctorates. Raised in a scientific and theoretical atmosphere, nurtured on contracts and grants from government agencies whose interests are different from those of the civilian market place, and mostly without industrial experience of their own, they cannot be expected to teach in a way that represents the whole spectrum of engineering.

Although present engineering graduates can do some things much better than the graduates of earlier generations, they have had little contact with the real world of engineering. They are better able to analyze problems that have been given them than to create new things; better able to work under direction than to give leadership in meeting the needs of society; hesitant to jump into uncharted areas; and relatively uninterested in the part of engineering that involves anticipating human needs or optimizing designs that involve costs, reliability, product life, manufacturability, salability, and acceptability.

* This chapter, as well as the next, is based on the work of a panel whose members were Robert B. Banks, Fred J. Benson, Donald L. Bitzer, William Bollay, R. E. Bolz, David R. Boylan, C. Stark Draper, S. B. Hammond, Ivan R. Hershner, John M. Ide, Vincent H. Larson, Joseph Liston, George D. Lobingier, S. M. Marco, Ralph G. Nevins, John A. Stephens, B. Richard Teare.

It is true that some of the best graduates rise above their education or supplement it on their own initiative and do become good creative engineers. However, many remain what their training has made them, differential-equation technicians. With a differently conceived education that gave them breadth beyond engineering science, that helped them learn how to deal with the whole range of their professional work, and that put greater emphasis on creativity, more of them would become engineering leaders. More of them would contribute importantly to technology and, finally, more would help make technology contribute significantly to society.

Thus, a major task facing educators today is to find out what this different and better kind of education may be and how to provide it. A number of promising methods are discussed by Professors Bolz and Dean in a later chapter. Most of them are characterized by an element of reality. Many schools are already using various combinations of these methods. However, even with the use of these methods, one cannot help having doubts as to whether what is being done is truly optimal. After all, if dealing with real-life situations were the only criterion of value, students might better find this part of their education in industry rather than the university, as many present graduates of necessity must do. In any case, some real-life situations provide better education than others; some accomplish one thing, while others have different purposes. It is the task of the university, in this area of education as in others, to frame specific educational objectives, and then consider the extent to which they are met by each of a variety of available methods and materials, so that these can be structured into a reasonably optimal program. A teacher should think in terms of these objectives and the extent to which any particular text, laboratory exercise, problem, case, or project fulfills them. This should be the basis for choosing among the materials, and modifying them if needed.

EDUCATIONAL AIMS

If we were to list some of the specific abilities and characteristics that are not well developed in present engineering programs, we might come up with such items as the recognition of problems, the identification of important elements in a situation, failure-mode analysis, cost consciousness, the concept of optimization, knowing how and when to approximate, knowing what makes people tick, the capacity to handle large complex problems, and so on through a long list of factors. From such a list we can devise a set of specific educational objectives for a program to help students develop their potential for creative engineering. We might outline them as follows.

1. *The Recognition and Formulation of Problems*

(a) Engineering students should be able to find problems in situations. They should have a sense of the urgency of looking for problems, rather than waiting until they are assigned. At the highest levels, graduates should be able to think creatively with respect to the multi-disciplinary problems, such as those concerning transportation, air and water pollution, information-handling systems, housing, and energy and material handling.

(b) Understanding the problem requires:

—Asking pertinent questions
—Sensing what is important
—Making realistic assumptions
—Relating to other similar problems
—Thinking in terms of analogies

2. *The Ability to Use the Full Range of Engineering Methods*

(a) Through the ability to choose. Graduates should be able to choose a suitable method from a wide range that varies from the simple to the sophisticated. For example:

—Reliability and other probability-based procedures
—Optimizing techniques
—Simulation and modeling
—Iterative techniques
—Trial and error approaches
—Decision-making techniques

Each method has a place in the engineer's arsenal, and he should recognize that the time available to deal with a problem often is a very important factor to consider in selecting a method.

(b) Through creative techniques for generating alternatives, including such methods as brain storming and metaphorical analogizing.*

* See Chapter 12.

(c) Through the gathering of information :
—From written sources : books, journals, reports
—From people
—From nature itself
—From experiment

Graduates should know how to get information from libraries and should be able to use modern methods of information retrieval. They should be able, also, to turn to the laboratory and get answers from nature and should not hesitate to do so when appropriate.

(d) Through the over-all testing of solutions. Engineers should habitually check their results by all suitable methods (for example, by letting variables approach critical limiting values or even by crude rule-of-thumb measures).

(e) Through imaginative use of the computer. Graduates should thoroughly understand the use of the computer, not only for calculation and simulation, but for other innovative uses, such as in computer-aided design, computer retrieval of information, and optimizing techniques. These are examples of innovative adaptations that have already been made. The full potential of the computer in education is not yet known and many more innovations are possible for creative engineering education.

3. *A Consciousness of Values and Costs*

Graduates should have a greater consciousness of social and economic values and the ability to deal with costs. It should be second nature for them to think of cost in relation to benefits and missions. They should understand trade-offs between capital and operating costs and should be able to estimate engineering costs for projects.

4. *An Appreciation of the Process of Innovation*

Graduates should be aware of what is involved in the innovative process, its importance to the growth of enterprises, and its central role in the growth of the economy.*

5. *A Cognizance of the Human Factors in Engineering*

Graduates must be aware of human problems and have a start toward competency in dealing with them. Understanding and work-

---

* See Chapter 14.

ing with people is one of the most important facets of the engineer's job. An engineering task sooner or later involves other people, usually both within and outside of the organization in which the engineer works. Often the human element is a key factor and he must be aware that this is so. Graduates must develop the ability to communicate, to sell ideas, and to understand and appreciate what it is that motivates others.

6. *A Critical Point of View*

Although much of what we have already outlined involves attitude, we should specifically note the need for a critical point of view regarding the status quo. This requires, among other things:

—The challenging of presuppositions
—Continually seeking improvements
—Keen powers of observation
—Insight

7. *A Capability for Self-development*

Graduates must think about their own place in the profession and the place of the profession in the world. They must plan what they will do to develop themselves to realize their full potential. In short, they should have:

—The ability to relate themselves to the world
—An awareness of the psychology of creativeness
—A plan for continuing education
—A program for keeping up with advances in science and technology.

OBJECTIVES AS STANDARDS

The objectives we have outlined can serve as a basis for analyzing and testing methods and materials proposed for creative engineering education. For example, design case materials may help to attain certain of these objectives, but not others; histories of the innovative process may meet some of the criteria not met by the cases, and so on. The testing of materials and methods in this way would be of assistance in deciding which to employ in order to accomplish the objectives of creative education.

Certain qualifying observations should be made. In the first place, it may be that not all engineering students should be offered the same program. Perhaps some should have what is basically the present program with only a slight modification in the direction of creative engineering, while others should be offered a program that has a great deal of creative engineering, even at the cost of extra time.

Second, different universities will have different sets of objectives. Educational institutions naturally value highly the freedom of selecting their own criteria. This diversity is salutary, for it avoids putting education in a strait jacket, promotes mutation and evolution, and helps to serve the demands of students and employers which are by no means uniform.

Thus, the set of educational objectives we have outlined is illustrative, not comprehensive. As such, it can be made the basis of further discussions directed toward the improvement of engineering education. Certainly, educational materials and methods should be evaluated in terms of specific educational objectives rather than the vague generalizations which often characterize discussions of creative engineering.

CHAPTER 10

THE MOTIVATION AND DEVELOPMENT OF FACULTY*

ROBERT B. BANKS

THE ability of any engineering school to provide a creative education depends primarily upon the abilities of its faculty members. These abilities are a function of interest and competence. Interest, in turn, stems from motivation; and competence for truly creative contributions to engineering education depends on the extent to which a teacher's past or present institution has prepared him for these ends by encouraging the development of the necessary traits.

In a word, then, the ability of an engineering teacher to become (and the likelihood of his becoming) a creative engineering educator depends upon the *motivation* and *development* policies and programs of his institution.

MOTIVATION OF FACULTY

There are different kinds of motivation. One is internal, or self-motivation; a second is external, or group motivation. Group motivation is reflected in the attitude and policy of an educational institution's administration toward the attainment of goals by means of the combined talents and efforts of its faculty.

In university life, as in so many walks of life, encouragement of individual efforts is reflected in promotions and salary increases. Generally, in universities, such advancements in rank or remuneration are made on the basis of contributions in teaching, in research, and in service to the university. As we all know, service to the universities is reflected in the work associated with long hours of committee duties, high-school visitations, community affairs, talks

---

* This chapter is based on the work of the panel identified in Chapter 9.

at professional meetings, and an almost endless list of other responsibilities. We all know about these collateral activities, expect them, and seek them to varying degrees. Let us look, therefore, at two main factors that are considered when advancement in rank and increases in salary are under review: teaching and research.

It is abundantly clear that involvement in research is the predominant factor. If any real and positive advances are to be made in creative engineering education, university administrators need to develop new and more appropriate yardsticks for the measurement of faculty accomplishments. The all-too-easy evaluation for promotion on the basis of publication of research results must be attenuated, though certainly not eliminated. Efforts should be amplified to identify and reward outstanding contributions in classroom and laboratory teaching. Within the framework of engineering education, a broader definition of "research" should be defined and accepted. For example, at both the master's and doctoral level, the supervision of theses which possess a tone of creative design, synthesis, development, field studies, and other "real world" involvements should be accepted and recognized by university administrators as on a par with the supervision of the more abstract and analytical graduate student endeavours that are now mainly pursued.

In teaching activities, particularly for undergraduates, sincere and meaningful support and recognition of engineering faculty must be made for efforts and achievements in the development of new teaching methods, course concepts, and curriculum directions. This is not a proposal to cast all faculty members into the same mold. Clearly, such an attempt would not be in the best interest of creative education. Rather, it is proposed that a broad spectrum of interests, talents, and inclinations be encouraged and maintained in a given engineering faculty.

To obtain a lasting and deep-seated *interest* of faculty members in the development of more creativity in engineering, it is imperative that they be *motivated* to acquire such an interest. As has already been pointed out, such motivation is not likely to be achieved unless university administrators clearly and unmistakably relate promotion and salary advances to meaningful contributions to creative engineering education. Thus, what is the attitude of a college dean or university administrator regarding the value of a faculty member's work for more creative engineering education?

How will his perhaps fewer and possibly less sophisticated published papers be recognized and evaluated?

Beyond these questions and considerations are others which may be even more difficult to resolve. First, there is the peer-group attitude. How is the faculty member who strives to instill a more creative spirit in engineering education accepted and recognized by his colleagues in the university? From the viewpoint of those more inclined toward theory and analysis, does creative design represent an appropriate function of a university?

Second, there is the universal problem of time. Teaching loads must be light enough to allow new course and curriculum development. Student–teacher ratios should be low enough to permit meaningful relationships with students. Encouragement needs to be given to the faculty to devote sabbatical leaves and summer periods to work in industry or at other universities in projects and programs bearing on creative engineering.

Third, faculty members should be encouraged to publish the results of their observations and experiences in creative engineering education. Such education would thereby be given additional emphasis and the relative paucity of information on the subject would be alleviated. Moreover, nation-wide motivation for more creativity in engineering education would be helped by such information transfer.

Finally, it is urged that as much collateral assistance as possible be given to faculty members. They should be given adequate clerical and stenographic help, shop and laboratory personnel, graduate student assistants, and appropriate budgets to keep up with related work at other institutions.

DEVELOPMENT OF FACULTY

The degree to which any real and positive advances can be made in creative engineering education is dependent on the competence of an engineering faculty for creative endeavors, which, in turn, depends upon institutional policies for developing such competence.

Such development may be aided in a number of ways.

—Faculty, particularly younger faculty, should be invited to attend special summer institutes which focus on creative engineering and in which industry-based people participate.
—Sabbatical leaves aimed at acquiring meaningful experience in

design, development, and production activities in industry should be encouraged.

—Arrangements should be made with companies and government agencies to develop summer employment programs for engineering faculty.

—Universities should encourage consulting activities by engineering faculty members, consistent with their teaching responsibilities.

—There should be an increased use of part-time instructors from industry.

—Faculty from other disciplines, especially from economics and business, should be brought in to conduct special seminars for engineering faculty and students.

—"Traveling Professorships" should be established to permit recognized leaders in creative engineering education to visit engineering campuses and discuss the techniques, problems, and opportunities involved in creative instruction.

THE COUPLED ASPECTS OF MOTIVATION AND DEVELOPMENT

There is an interaction between the *motivation* and the *development* of faculty to work for a more creative kind of engineering education. The encouragement of experimentation in new teaching methods simultaneously motivates and develops. The use of case methods in engineering education is an example. It has been observed that positive and optimistic attitudes regarding the use of such methods are evinced when desires to develop new courses and new curricula based on these methods are encouraged.

At the post-graduate level, faculty members should be encouraged to develop much more activity in design and synthesis-oriented graduate student theses. To enhance the likelihood that the marked imbalance in favour of theoretical, analysis-oriented theses may be reduced, it would appear more appropriate for an engineering college, instead of an associated graduate college, to have control over all aspects of the education of graduate students in engineering.

In summary, the success of the efforts proposed here regarding creative engineering education will depend primarily upon the programs and policies which universities maintain with respect to the motivation and development of faculty. University administrators can retard or stop advances in this mission by giving lip-service endorsement to the concept, but failing, for instance, to approve promotions or significant salary increases for deserving faculty.

It should be noted, too, that in the absence of substantial support for these efforts on the part of government, industry, and the foundations, inadequate progress will be made. For unless these sources of support provide assistance approaching a par with their support of basic research endeavors, no long-lasting or significant advances will occur in creative engineering education. If we are to attain the goals we seek, the proper environment and resources must be made available for the motivation and the development of engineering educators.

CHAPTER II

STRATEGIES AND TEACHING METHODS

RAY E. BOLZ AND ROBERT C. DEAN, JR.

UNDERGRADUATE engineering education and, to a great extent, graduate education, are primarily concerned with two objectives: the acquisition and understanding of knowledge, and the development of the skill of analysis of problems concerning physical science and engineering. What the educational experience almost completely excludes is the exercise and development of the students' creativity—even though creativity is probably the single most important characteristic demanded of a modern, practicing engineer. One may argue, in view of the great developments of technology in the United States, that our educational pattern in engineering has been successful. However, whether this pattern will continue indefinitely to be successful in a more competitive world is doubtful. In any case, we could do better if we were to develop better methods in our educational programs for bringing out the creative ability of students.

Success in reaching this most difficult goal would, we believe, increase the motivation of our students in such a significant way as to result in a greater acquisition of knowledge, understanding, and analytical ability. This could be achieved, even though the actual time devoted to these formalistic aspects of education were somewhat reduced in favour of increasing the emphasis and time devoted to activities of a creative nature.

The purpose of this chapter is to propose several strategies for enhancing the development of creative engineering education and to recommend a variety of teaching methods which we believe could contribute significantly to building the creative powers of engineer-

STRATEGIES AND TEACHING METHODS

ing students.* Such methods have one common denominator; they require the student to face problems that require ingenuity, inventiveness, and decisions regarding competing alternatives. Let us turn now to a consideration, first, of several teaching methods and materials and, then, of strategies for the development of creative engineering education.

TEACHING METHODS AND MATERIALS

Case Studies

Case studies have been employed extensively in legal, business, and medical education. In engineering, however, the case method of study has been used sparingly and often ineffectively.

The case study method requires certain ingredients, including the

(a) selection of problems from actual industrial experience, demonstrating a new design, process or system and exhibiting a recognized creative contribution,
(b) preparation and documentation of the steps in the solution of the problem, done in close cooperation with the engineers who accomplished the work,
(c) proper presentation of the problem (not the solution),
(d) requirement that the students as individuals or teams first attack the problem and devise their own solution,
(e) presentation of the actual solution or solutions, and
(f) evaluation of the students' solutions in light of those actually used.

The writing of case studies is difficult, time-consuming and costly, and requires experienced professionals to accomplish a successful job. Moreover, case studies must be changed from year to year at any one school, although the same case—if it still represents modern engineering—can be presented after a lapse of several years. Hence, a national effort to create an ample and continuous supply of case

* This chapter is based on the recommendations of a conference subgroup which, in addition to the authors, comprised Robert B. Banks, Fred J. Benson, Donald L. Bitzer, William Bollay, Carl W. Borgmann, David R. Boylan, C. Stark Draper, Newman A. Hall, S. B. Hammond, Ivan R. Hershner, James R. Hooper, John M. Ide, Harry S. Kantor, William C. Kelly, Vincent H. Larson, Robert H. Linnell, Joseph Liston, George D. Lobingier, S. M. Marco, J. W. Mason, David C. Miller, Ralph G. Nevins, Andrew S. Schultz, William Shockley, John A. Stephens, R. Richard Teare, Ralph Trese, Karl H. Vesper, Brooks Walker.

studies is required. It should be noted that Stanford University has begun to work in this direction.

The method used for presentation of these cases is important and may take a variety of forms. Suggested methods include oral presentation with visual aids, taped presentation with slides or films, and written presentation as a reading assignment. Industrial experts should be invited to help organize and present cases that arise from their creative solutions of actual industrial problems. Where feasible, this technique is most effective. The use of graduate students to prepare design cases in fulfillment of their theses problems at the master's level is an intriguing possibility. Whatever the technique, however, it should be understood that implementation of the case method will be difficult, for it requires the development of broad faculty interest and involvement in case studies as a teaching device.

Case Histories

We suggest the publication of case history books that describe in considerable detail examples of successful creative activities by engineers. The books might be prepared under the supervision of an ad hoc committee and distributed through engineering departments in the universities.

Inspirational Literature

Students should also have an opportunity to read books that not only describe the role of the engineer, but project that role into the future and relate it to the development of our society. We suggest:

1. Preparation of a bibliography for this purpose. Biographies, auto-biographies, descriptions of important projects involving failures and successes. The American Society for Engineering Education or the Commission on Engineering Education, in cooperation with publishers, might stimulate this activity.
2. Encouragement of the writing of competently done "engineering fiction", similar to "science fiction", but emphasizing creative imagination in engineering. Prizes by book publishers might be used to generate these materials; support might come from industry, government and foundations.

Projects for Students

The project method offers an excellent opportunity for the exercise and development of creativity, although many so-called project courses fall far short of the goal. Projects for students may include small design projects, broad interdisciplinary projects, laboratory projects, and open-ended problems. The success of any of these depends upon the fulfillment of one basic criterion: does the project, whether broad or narrow, require at least one creative contribution on the part of the student?

Implementation of meaningful project work is much more difficult than may appear because any successful project needs to be a new experience for the student. Furthermore, it must be bounded so that it is within both the student's capability to handle and the time limits of the course of study. Other factors include available equipment, funds for miscellaneous expenses, and faculty time, of which much is required.

Problems of implementation, beyond those already mentioned, center around questions of the difficulty of injecting the "real world" into the university environment, of reward and recognition of the faculty who participate and provide the unusual effort and time required for a successful and continuing project program, and of satisfying the need for critical, experienced guidance and evaluation of the project during its progress and at the termination of the work. With respect to the last of these factors, the use of projects of industrial origin, and industrial designers as consultants playing an active role in the conduct and review of the work, could contribute significantly to success.

Motivation for the students and faculty could be enhanced by competition among project teams both on a school basis as well as on a national basis.

Student Internships—Summer or Co-op

Coupled with other programs, the proper use of the summer periods in a four-year academic program or of the co-op work-experience periods in a five-year program is an excellent educational plan for engineering students. However, merely setting aside such periods or organizing a co-op program does not solve the problem. Success depends critically on several factors. First, the selection of the projects must be made with great care in order to fulfill almost all of the requirements previously discussed for projects. Second, the industries involved must be willing to invest a significant portion of the time and effort of their creative design and development engineers who, as project guides, must insist that the students conduct the project and not merely carry out the ideas and suggestions of their mentors. Third, each co-op project ideally should also have a faculty consultant associated with it who would take an active, part-time role in the conduct of the project in its industrial environment.

"Forefront" Engineering Activity on the College Campus

Engineering schools should develop programs of professional, creative engineering work involving the solution of advanced design problems, systems problems, and new process or product problems. These programs could be aimed at public or social problems, including pollution, resource conservation, highway safety, and other such areas where government laboratories are active and where no direct competition with industry is involved. Such programs could be financed with government funds in the way that basic research programs in science are now supported. These activities could be associated with engineering schools the way hospital activities are associated with medical schools.

Some of the problems that need be overcome for success of such programs (other than funding) have to do with the nature of the academic world. The activity described would usually not lead to publications and, therefore, there would be the problem of acceptance by faculties and administrators and, in turn, problems of recognition and promotion. More important is the recognition of the "tightrope" that must be walked between an activity such as described and the province of profit-oriented industry. Perhaps engineering schools could be integrated with nonprofit research and development laboratories similar to those which have long been associated, in name at least, with a number of universities. Such integration would require that the research and development laboratory and engineering school share common goals of education and creative engineering output.

An important adjunct of this lab–school partnership would be a changed concept of graduate theses. Encouraging, and on most campuses even permitting, graduate theses to deal with the design of new and novel systems, products and processes would greatly help in creating a favorable climate for the rise in "forefront" engineering activity on the campus.

Campus-centered Commercial Ventures

Real-life problems could also be brought to the university through establishment of a campus-centered commercial venture, organized with industrial and faculty guidance and run by graduate students, but providing employment possibilities for all levels of the undergraduate program as well. The primary teaching mission of the program may introduce problems in making it self-financing, but the net cost may be a cheap price for the experience provided. The school paper and yearbook have been run along these lines on many campuses for many years. Consequently, the extension of such activities to engineering-oriented ventures may not be as radical as appears at first glance. Industrial participation can be as varied and extensive as local conditions permit; subcontract work is a possibility, and cooperation with the business schools can further extend the scope of the program.

STRATEGIES

We should note at the outset that no strategy will provide greater motivation to a student to be creative than will creative activities in his educational experience. The teaching methods and materials we have discussed are directed to this end. We turn now to a consideration of several strategies which, in our view, would further enhance the development of creative engineering education.

A Market Survey

We suggest a market survey of employers of engineers which, in effect, would ask: "How much creativity do you want? What level of creative effort is required in each segment of your engineering work force?" These data should be made available to the academic institutions as an aid to them in their planning process. Further, this information should be made available at regular intervals—perhaps every three to five years—so that engineering institutions can obtain reasonably prompt feedback on the impact of new educational programs. We recommend that some responsible national organization, such as the National Academy of Engineering, the American Society for Engineering Education, or the Commission on Engineering Education, assume the responsibility for making this survey.

Enhancement of the "Image" of the Creative Person

The public, and especially the students, should be given an opportunity to learn the facts about the modern creative engineer. The humanities have been more successful in demonstrating the joys of creative life than have the sciences and engineering. We suggest:

1. Films and TV presentations of "Lives of the Creative Engineers" similar to those on lives of the artists.
2. Increased effort to show the responsibility and social impact of the engineer in important national programs. TV coverage of space missions, bringing out the *engineer's* role, is an example.

Appeal to Idealism of Students

The education of engineering students should be related to the social problems of the day. We suggest the development of lists of simple inventions—for example, devices needed by Peace Corpsmen in their work. These lists should be made available to engineering undergraduates and solutions could be solicited by an ad hoc committee or by the Peace Corps directly.

Identification of Creative Talent

Different types of training probably best serve engineers headed for different types of career roles. It may not be that all students should receive the same relative emphasis on the development of creativeness. Nevertheless, exceptionally creative individuals should be sought out and cultivated. To accomplish this, we note the following possibilities.

1. *Systematic studies*—directed toward the identification of the characteristics of creative engineers and toward the development of tests to predict creative performance in professional work. Much work has been carried on by educational psychologists and others. We recommend continuation of this effort, but in greater cooperation with engineering teachers. Special attention should be given to the characteristics of inventors.

2. *Identification during "creative" activities.* Creative activities involving case studies, internships, and other realistic experiences can serve as a medium for evaluating the creativity of individuals. The good "performer" in "creative" school activities is probably

above average in creative ability. If activities could pervade engineering education and not be limited to junior and senior undergraduates, the identification of exceptionally creative individuals could begin in school.

3. *National competitions* can be an effective means of stimulating and recognizing talented individuals. Examples of such programs are

—The national invention competitions of the National Inventors Council, U.S. Department of Commerce. The most recent national competition was for a stair-climbing wheelchair. New areas for such competitions should be explored.
—The high-school talent searches and Science Fairs of Science Service, supported by the Westinghouse Corporation. Although these programs stress elegant analytical problem solving, they could be modified for college students and be aimed at engineering instead of science.

4. *College placement offices* should be alerted to developments in creative engineering education and encouraged to make use of faculty evaluations of the creative propensity of students.

5. *Fellowship selection procedures* should be reviewed (especially those at the national level) to make sure that they recognize and encourage, rather than de-emphasize and discourage, creativity.

Communication Among Schools

Many different techniques for enhancing creativity *already exist*. Most of them have already been tried somewhere and many of them are presently in use at one school or another. But many are unknown to other schools. For schools to profit by the experience of others, improved communication of these experiences is necessary. The American Society for Engineering Education should take the lead in ascertaining what is being done in the field of creative engineering education and make this information available to the public. In addition, it would be extremely valuable to institute:

—A continuing program of summer conferences on the teaching of creative engineering education.
—A system of lectureships on such teaching.
—Faculty exchange programs to spread creative educational know-how.

School Administrations

As Professor Banks has indicated in his essay, the pivotal factor in the development of creative engineering education is the sympathetic and active participation of school administrations. As to the faculty, once the administration of an institution has decided to balance its program in the direction of increased emphasis on creativity, it becomes necessary to develop faculty appreciation of the need to support such a program. This can be partially accomplished by influencing existing members, particularly the younger group, and partly by the selection process inherent in new faculty appointments. In any case, the desired change will require appropriate rewards both in salary and rank for contributions to the program. This applies to existing faculty as well as new members who may be brought in.

We recognize that the problem of evaluating and suitably rewarding teaching contributions is an old and thorny one, but we point out that what we are proposing is the rewarding of creative effort —research and development in the educational process.

Since it would not be practicable to staff such an effort predominantly with new faculty members, it will be necessary to retrain and reorient a substantial element of the existing faculties of many institutions. This can be accomplished through training programs or by significant industrial experience. Academic administrators should therefore work to establish a climate which will be attractive to such reoriented faculty members and to others who may join the staff.

Greater efforts should also be made to encourage existing members of faculties to obtain significant industrial experience. While short-term employment such as summer work and consulting on technical specialities is helpful, we feel that major benefits will occur only through longer periods of involvement of faculty members in responsible engineering work. In this connection we urge a continuation and expansion of such activities as the Ford Foundation program of residencies in engineering practice.

Other Influential Factors

In addition to the factors we have outlined for improving the environment for creative engineering education are the following, some of which are obvious, though others may not be so apparent:

—A strong and persistent call from industry for more creative engineers.

— Pressure from faculty members for opportunities to teach and learn creative engineering.
— The demands of students, particularly as demonstrated by popularity of any creativity-oriented courses.
— Pressure from alumni, foundations, government, philanthropists.
— A change in the criteria for accreditation of engineering schools, so that creative engineering instruction is given substantial emphasis.
— Enlistment of the active support of well-known and influential people.
— The use of engineering faculty to staff government summer projects on problems of state, regional or national concern.
— The availability of government and foundation grants to teachers who want to experiment with creative engineering education, especially teachers in schools without a prior history of grants.
— The establishment of a national award for "the creative engineering teacher of the year".

CONCLUSIONS

We believe that certain deficiencies are manifest in engineering education, that useful remedies are known, and that the principal problem is to get individuals and organizations to act on them. The ideas expressed here center on the fundamental proposition that creativity in engineering students can be developed most effectively by inviting them to engage in creative activities.

Encouraging inquisitiveness and creative involvement should be an objective in every engineering course. Few would question the desirability of this goal. Yet, its attainment would involve a revolution in most of our engineering teaching methods and materials, for present teaching programs generally concentrate on imparting knowledge and developing analytical abilities. The development of inquisitiveness and creative capacity, on the other hand, involves such things as self-discovery, hard decisions in multiple-solution situations, the modeling of real-world situations, and the process of synthesis. If each engineering school course and laboratory were revised to include opportunities for these kinds of inquiring activities, creative engineers would be more common. Although the obstacles that stand in the way of such changes are numerous and formidable, they are not insurmountable. With some compromises, and the active and sympathetic support of key groups in industry and government and, most of all, in the universities, they could be overcome.

DISCUSSION

Educational Engineering

CARL VESPER: My job at Stanford has been mainly to introduce and to try experiments with the case method of teaching. I've been an "educational engineer", you might say; I'm supposed to play a sort of transfer role. Before I started working at Stanford I worked at the Harvard Business School using cases. I therefore came to Stanford with a tool that was familiar to me, even though I had used it in business administration and not in engineering. But it was a tool which was not familiar to the faculty in the engineering department at Stanford—and that posed the most difficult problem, because the real difficulty in the case system is not the preparation and composition of cases, but getting the instructor to try them in ways which probably conflict with his established patterns.

One of these patterns, found in most engineering professors, is the habit of pontificating. They have all the answers, and they dole them out to the students at a steady pace. But the case method calls for a different way of teaching and, therefore, a modification of established habits. It can be done, but it takes a great deal of determination and quite a bit of time. It is worth it, though, to any teacher really interested in giving students creative experiences instead of steady doses of answers and analytical problems.

Example Teaches

WILLIAM SHOCKLEY: Case problems and histories are very effective and the reason is one that underlies all processes of education. I would like to demonstrate the theory that is involved here. [He rolls several newspapers into a tight, club-like configuration.]

The theory, in a nutshell, is that *example teaches*. [He loudly pounds a table with the rolled newspaper.] There is nothing that teaches more effectively and memorably than a dry [BANG], exaggerated [BANG], example [BANG]! That is the power of the case history [BANG], because dramatized examples get attention. We remember them because they are aimed directly at the retentive features of the human brain.

Science and Technology in a Larger System

EDGAR L. PIRET: We have discussed strategies for improving engineering education. It is interesting to note who among the academic groups are doing most of the creative work in starting programs and trying to learn something about the interactions of science and technology with the political, economic, and social problems of the nation; they are not on the faculties of engineering. As far as I can tell, they are primarily on the faculties of political science, public administration, and business administration. Although the concern about these interactions of science and technology is an immensely important area, it is one in which hardly any competence or interest has been demonstrated by the engineering schools. There is much to be done to fill this void.

CHAPTER 12

EDUCATING PROSPECTIVE INVENTORS

JACOB RABINOW

I HAVE discussed the process of invention at length in a previous chapter.* In this chapter I shall outline the findings and recommendations of a panel on the teaching of invention, of which I was privileged to serve as chairman.† As has already been noted, creativity involves the discovery of new concepts and relationships, new products and processes. The process of invention, a creative art, is primarily concerned with engineering, but the techniques we shall consider may also be of interest to the fine arts and other disciplines.

Our panel was unanimous in the belief that creativity can be taught, and that the national creative output can be markedly increased by a conscious and deliberate effort to provide a more encouraging environment in our homes and schools and in industry. To achieve these ends our panel made a number of recommendations which are classified below, first in terms of their general applicability, and then according to their applicability to the high-school or college level.

GENERAL

The creative act has been associated with the scientific method, the logical deduction of solutions, keen observation, analogous reasoning, random searching, the deliberate effort to find an unexpected solution, and other mental processes. Our panel recommended that continuing research be focused on these processes.

The identification of creative individuals is difficult, and no

* See Chapter 6.
† Other members of the panel were Hugh Bradner, Leonard S. Hardland, James L. Massey, William B. McLean, Howard O. McMahon, George M. Prince, Leon Robbin, Samuel Ruben, C. D. W. Thornton, Richard R. Walton.

simple or reliable tests are known. We felt, therefore, that no attempt should be made to select and segregate creative students at the grade-school level. All children should be given as much encouragement as possible to develop their creative potential, for an encouraging environment seems to be the best way of bringing forth the creative individual.

Traits such as curiosity, a questioning attitude, and originality should be expressly recognized and encouraged at all levels of grade school, high school, and college. The primary hindrance to creativity at all levels of education is the grading system, which rewards faith in and adherence to dogma. Grades or other recognition should be given for creativity. There is no reason, for example, why creativity cannot be an additional factor in supplementary ratings such as those for effort, behavior, and attendance.

Since creativity is an individualistic phenomenon, the recognition and encouragement of creativeness must be done on an individual basis. Therefore, much smaller classes would be highly desirable at all levels of school. This is particularly important with regard to creativity because it is a latent talent which is difficult to bring forth. Moreover, the advancement of teachers should depend heavily on the stimulating quality of their teaching.

HIGH SCHOOL

High schools should make efforts to obtain experienced engineers and, if possible, experienced creative engineers to teach science courses. It should be the aim of these schools to impart to students a knowledge of the non-academic world of science. The use of television instruction for this purpose would be unsatisfactory; but television does have an important use as a supplement—for example, to acquaint students with special features, large projects, important personalities, and as a career guidance stimulus.

In order to attract creative engineers to teach in high-school programs, salaries should be raised to make these positions competitive with professional salaries in business, government, and the universities.

High-school students have only a vague knowledge of what the engineering profession is, and practically no concept of creative engineering. To correct this, it is recommended that creative professionals from local industry and government be invited to meet and talk with students at appropriate times during the school year.

COLLEGE

Student creativity should be rewarded by grades or some other form of recognition at the college level. This is important for stimulating creativity; it would also be useful for getting measures of the effectiveness of a creative engineering program.

The life histories of the great inventors and innovators lead one to conclude that individual encouragement of students by dedicated professors is probably the most important single factor in developing creativity in school. Accordingly, our panel made the following recommendations:

—Specialists in the techniques of creativity should be used to give courses to teachers and to selected students.
—Good creative people should be borrowed from industry for a semester or more to instruct classes which stress creativity.
—Central agencies or societies should maintain rosters of good speakers on subjects of creative engineering.
—Special courses in creativity should, if at all possible, be taught by men at the peak of their creative careers.

Case problems of current industrial or government interest should be made the basis for creative engineering classes in design. These problems should be real and should not have known, satisfactory solutions. They should be challenging to both the teacher and the student. The students should be told that a good invention is only a beginning, that other inventions have to be conceived to protect the basic idea. It should be noted that simpler problems could be used at the high-school level. Perhaps these could be solved problems rather than unsolved ones.

It may be advisable, as part of teaching creativity, to teach some real-world legal and economical aspects, such as patents, legal and proprietary rights, trade secrets, professional ethics of engineers, international patent aspects, contract matters between employer and employee, and so on. With regard to involving patents, it should be recognized that inventors, like other people, may forget or distort the historical record of their inventions. Therefore, it is particularly important that teachers and students keep careful records of the sequence of thoughts in problem projects. The steps in the creative process should be examined and recorded with as much care as the steps in the technical solution.

Additional techniques for developing the creative potential of engineering students include activities to develop an understanding of the process of thinking, to develop the attitude, "It's possible", and to develop the power of observation. Let us discuss examples of each of these.

DEVELOPING AN UNDERSTANDING OF THE THINKING PROCESS

Because thoughts and ideas develop with great speed and in generally unknown ways within the human mind, few know *how* they attack a problem. An engineering class may develop a greater understanding of the problem-solving process if they are involved in an activity such as the following:

1. Divide the students into groups of not more than six.
2. Ask them to develop together a step-by-step outline of how they actually solve problems.
3. Give them a problem that is relatively simple to state, but very difficult to solve. (Devise a new circular saw blade that cuts wood, but not people.)
4. Tell them to use their outline to attack the problem together for one hour. Tape-record the proceedings.
5. Have the groups trade tapes and listen to another group's work. They should listen for *behavior*; i.e., did they follow their outline, did all agree on the problem, was there organization, was it effective, did ideas get "shot down" quickly, did one person build on another's ideas, did people listen to each other, etc. Each behavior should be noted.
6. Next, have each group listen to its own tape in the same fashion.
7. Ask each group to evaluate its own behaviors by classifying them as "desirable", "undesirable", or "don't know".
8. Instruct each group to devise a problem-solving procedure that will encourage the desirable behaviors and discourage the undesirables. The "don't knows" should be experimented with.
9. Finally, give the students a second problem and ask them to recycle steps 4–7. The procedure is repeated until the groups

have developed a procedure that is both helpful and capable of being followed.

The above activity could be included in a course using course material to supply problems. However, the problems should be difficult and without known satisfactory answers.

Developing the Attitude, "It's Possible"

One of the characteristics of an inventor is his conviction that if something does not operate to his satisfaction it is an opportunity; he can do something about it. To cultivate this attitude we must cultivate, first, an awareness of dissatisfaction and, second, the conviction that something can be done about it. The following method may be useful for cultivating these two characteristics.

1. On a weekly or monthly basis, have each student describe a situation he finds unsatisfactory—for example, finding it uncomfortable to get into a cold car on cold mornings.
2. Select the most intriguing problem or situation and assign it to the entire class for solution. It may be useful to divide the class into teams of three or four.
3. The team with the most elegant solution should then be asked to present it to the rest of the class.

Developing the Power of Observation

Another characteristic of an inventor is his habit of noticing the world around him and later making use of his observations. This habit of observation may be cultivated by:

1. Having each student visit a museum that contains artifacts from a primitive civilization. Tell him to select three artifacts that represent, to him, elegant solutions to a problem faced by that civilization (for example, bow and arrow, Eskimo harpoon, wedge). He should study and sketch each of his three selections.
2. Assigning each student the task of writing a dialogue for an imaginary problem-solving meeting at which one of the artifacts of his choice was invented.
3. Reading the two or three best dialogues to class.
4. Giving the same assignment in various environments other than a museum—for example, a "Five and Ten" store, a hardware store, a construction site, an automobile repair garage.

The above specific suggestions for developing the creative potential of engineering students are illustrative examples. Other techniques will occur to individual teachers of engineering. The important point is that creative characteristics exist to some degree in most people. By systematically and directly cultivating these traits, it should be possible to encourage each student to grow nearer his potential.

Special courses and workshops in creativity should be brought into the curriculum during summer school and through the medium of symposia, if possible. They should also be worked into regular courses. But the teaching of creativity should not be done at the expense of other essential subjects taught today. We are led to believe that four years of college is probably not enough to develop a good engineer in the modern world. It would be well worth while to support, at one or more colleges, a five-year engineering program stressing creative techniques and courses. Such concentration of effort and support would ensure the speedy and effective development of this concept of education.

In closing, it should be emphasized that there is nothing basically incompatible between the present engineering curricula and the above-listed proposals. They are directed to the encouragement of stronger, more conscious attitudes of creativity, inquiry, and invention. These attitudes are in keeping with the aims of engineering.

DISCUSSION

Observation

BROOKS WALKER: Every inventor I have known has been a very good observer. He will walk down the street with other people and he will see two or three things while he is walking a few blocks that the other people won't see. He will file these observations away and perhaps some time apply them to a perceived need. This power of observation is a very important characteristic of inventors, which can be nurtured and developed in our educational system.

Dissatisfaction

JACK MORTON: Jacob Rabinow tells of a trip he took once on the New York Thruway and his finding it tiresome to drive for long periods—his foot pushing on the gas pedal, his arm engaged with the steering wheel. So he went home and invented a method of avoiding this; it was an electronic system for following the car ahead of you or following the road. This illustrates a trait which is imbued in every inventor. Most people who are dissatisfied with a situation usually "react" by getting along with it; but inventors want to change it. It seems to me that this is something that can be taught if we are clever enough in going about it. Students, for example, might be asked to identify situations they are particularly dissatisfied with, to specify what they would do to improve upon the status quo, and to convince the class that their alternatives are indeed an improvement.

If this became an established habit, students would be learning, among other things, the art of the possible. They would be imbued with the very creative attitude that they do not have to accept things the way they are.

Size of Classes

COSTAS ANAGNOSTOPOULOS: Smaller classes are, it seems to me, an essential precondition to effective education for creativity.

C. STARK DRAPER: In my quizzes about 80 per cent of the questions are such that, if students have studied their lessons well and absorbed the requisite knowledge, they can pass. The other 20 per cent are not questions; they are situations containing no specific problems. The students are asked to deal with these situations. The problem for them is that they have to formulate their own problems.

I find it unproductive to try to take the "brilliant" students and put them in separate sections. I let them select themselves. I have found that a certain percentage—roughly 20 to 30 per cent—will be challenged by the "situation" kind of question. It is, as I have noted, not a problem at all. It is something to think about, and out of the whole class a minority will attempt to solve it. You see, students don't have to solve these to get by in the course. But these kinds of questions give me an opportunity to see who the potential inventors and innovators are; and the size of my "creative" classes is therefore determined by a kind of natural selection process. Instead of having over-all small classes, I have what you might call a super small class of discussions with the few students who have picked up these impossible "situation" questions and attempted to do something imaginative about them. The interesting thing to me has been that the people who are attracted (or annoyed) by these questions turn out to be the more imaginative students, and the more "situations" I give them, the more adept they become in dealing with them. As they go along, I give them more and more complex situations and then I just talk to them about their reactions.

This, I think, is a sort of automatic way of getting a small class.

JACOB RABINOW: Students who do badly in large classes in public schools sometimes are sent to private schools. Apparently, they do much better in private schools, for two reasons. One is that the teachers are better, and the other is that the classes are much smaller.

Following Through on Inventions

JOSEPH LISTON: We should pay more attention to the follow-through on inventions made by students in our design courses. How can we keep the invention from becoming an anti-climax? We get a student fired up to do a job of creative work, but then let him run out of gas. Some kind of national clearinghouse for the better ideas as they come up would help to avoid this anti-climax.

Another possibility would be to use some kind of an "idea placement service" on the campuses. Most universities have a student placement service where the students are brought to the attention of potential employers at the time of their graduation. Why not a student idea placement service of

DISCUSSION

some kind, where their outstanding ideas could be made available to people in a position to follow up on them?

JACOB RABINOW: The question is, should we take a student invention all the way through to the real world? If you tell him, "Forget it, we don't want you to bother with it," it does dampen his creative talent. But if you want to play good tennis in a tournament, you have to practice playing tennis first, so the student should be told he is playing a practice game, which is perfectly useful, and that when he goes into industry he will have his opportunity to run in the real race.

ROBERT DEAN, JR.H Nevertheless, we should be trying in the classroom to develop realistic situations, and if a student knows that everything he comes up with will be shelved, he may lose enthusiasm. We should offer the student the encouragement that if he really creates something good, there is a way to continue.

DANIEL DE SIMONE: What Professor Liston was proposing, and Professor Dean was following up on, is how do you get some innovative follow-through, in appropriate cases, where at least an attempt ought to be made to mature an invention into an innovation. Professors Liston and Dean were asking how this could be done *some* of the time, not every time. They are proposing an escape valve for student inventions that are outstanding.

JOSEPH LISTON: The significant thing, it seems to me, is that the opportunity ought to exist whereby, occasionally, the student is not completely blocked.

HERBERT SHEPARD: If we want to imbue the student with a strong sense of realism, then the provision of a nice reward system would not be equipping him with the realism he should expect on the outside. An invention has to be very good to qualify for a patent, and then the next question is what do you do with the patent? Sometimes the most an inventor gets in the way of satisfaction is finding out that a really good man thought of this some years before. Students should not be led to expect more than reality affords.

LLOYD HATCH: I think the student should be encouraged along the lines suggested by Professor Liston. He should be informed of the many difficult steps that are required to bring even outstanding ideas to reality, and then he should be given at least an opportunity to explore the possibilities for his own idea. He would get a great deal of education out of it, and I'll bet the instructor would get an education out of it, too.

CHAPTER 13

PREPARING INNOVATORS AND ENTREPRENEURS

RICHARD S. MORSE[*]

THE innovative process is a complex system which is influenced by many factors. In a broad sense the innovative process includes such activities as the introduction of new procedures within a corporate or industrial structure, the development and exploitation of new products and processes, and the launching of technical enterprises.

In an effort to study the innovative process, and to identify important factors influencing its success or failure, we reviewed some case histories of innovative developments. As an example of an early, uncomplicated product development effort, consideration was given to the development, production and imagined distribution of the first clay pot by prehistoric men. This example illustrated fundamental aspects of a highly simplified operation and some important factors in the innovative process.

We also reviewed several modern industrial developments of a more complicated nature. These reviews included the histories of frozen orange juice, Krillium, artificial diamonds, the microwave maser, and thermoplastic recording. Some of these innovative efforts were highly successful; others were not.

In each of the histories we analyzed, we noted the importance of such nontechnical factors as marketing, production costs, and timing. In each instance the tremendous importance of a single "champion" for the project was clearly established, which indicated that factors of inspiration, stimulation and a feeling of enthusiastic commitment are essential ingredients of success. This is not to say that basic research is unessential; it is essential to the advance of

[*] Mr. Morse was chairman of a panel whose work formed the basis for this chapter. Other members of the panel were Costas E. Anagnostopoulos, Myron A. Coler, Jack C. Davis, Daniel V. De Simone, Michael P. Gaus, J. Herbert Hollomon, Fred Kremer, Jr., Jack A. Morton, Donald A. Schon, John C. Stedman, Lowell W. Steele.

science and technology. But the introduction of the results of science and technology into the market place is what ultimately determines economic growth and social welfare. The innovative process, therefore, is manifested in the successful introduction of new ideas in a commercial sense, and neither research nor the birth of a new idea is any more important than such nontechnical factors as marketing and the acquisition of venture capital.

Innovation as a total connected process is recognized by some industries, but the industrial and government climate, as a whole, is neither adequately appreciative of nor conducive to innovation in our society. It should be noted, too, that the need for innovation and a knowledge of the process are as essential to the universities and government as they are to the commercial sector of the economy.

There is a need in our educational system, at both the undergraduate and graduate levels, to become more aware of the significance of the innovative process and to treat it as a subject of special importance. The teaching of the innovative process, including the development of the creative characteristics of students, cannot effectively be accomplished by conventional academic methods, focused on single, nonintegrated disciplines.

Having considered some of the diverse elements of the innovative process, we may ask what capabilities an innovator must possess. In addition to imagination, drive, good judgment, a sense of timing, and other traits, he must have an adequate knowledge base. The educational process typically contributes to the knowledge base. However, the other characteristics of a true innovator are highly dependent upon the climate in which he has acquired knowledge, and it is hoped that progress can be made in the development of such traits by appropriate changes in the teaching process.

In particular, the following approaches are proposed:

1. Educational institutions, especially the engineering and business schools, should direct their attention to the innovative processes in an effort to develop new approaches to the teaching of innovation and entrepreneurship, and initiate research activities in this general area. It would seem that the most effective teaching technique would combine the learning process with actual practice, particularly at the graduate educational level.

2. Individuals experienced in problems of innovation and entre-

preneurship should be incorporated into the academic environment both as full-time faculty and members of the consulting staff. This infusion of experienced talent could have a salutary effect on the entire faculty.

3. In the area of entrepreneurship, emphasis should be put upon the direct association of students with the organization and management of new ventures, such work to be undertaken in collaboration with the faculty, industry, and the community.

4. The concept of an "industrial internship" teaching technique should be given serious consideration. Under this proposal, students would, in the sense of the medical intern, actually work in industrial companies that have demonstrated a capacity for innovation.

5. Educational institutions should recognize the need for an interdisciplinary approach to the teaching of innovation and bring to bear knowledge and experience in such areas as law, the social sciences, marketing, finance, and management techniques.

There are many skills and areas of knowledge regarding the innovative and entrepreneurial processes which can be taught. Among these skills and areas of knowledge are the following:

1. The problems of entrepreneurship.
2. The application of new technology.
3. Appraisal techniques for innovative ideas.
4. The evaluation of markets.
5. The generation of corporate support.
6. A realistic understanding of the corporate and industrial environments.
7. The availability and acquisition of venture capital.
8. The relation and impact of government policy.
9. The current and future impact of government research and development.
10. The cost–time–market–dynamics of the innovative process.
11. The interplay between technological, economic, and sociological trends.
12. The techniques of introducing innovation in society, industry, and government.
13. The management of the innovative process in both large and small corporations.
14. The relationships between large and small corporations.

To sum up, two principal teaching techniques are applicable to the education of students in the fields of innovation and entrepreneurship. The first involves analytical teaching procedures—in particular, the development of models of the innovative and entrepreneurial processes. These analytical methods can significantly aid in the development of understanding of the areas of skills and knowledge illustrated above.

The second technique for teaching innovation and entrepreneurship is the heuristic approach. It requires that the student experience, in a real or vicarious way, the problems and challenges of the innovative and entrepreneurial processes. Such experience can be provided through such means as business cases, internship programs, and actual student involvement in the formation of new corporate ventures.

In closing, it should be emphasized that the success of the kinds of teaching we propose will be dependent upon improved understanding of the innovative and entrepreneurial processes. In particular, what is needed is the development of a discipline in this field; our knowledge must have structure to be truly useful. The development of this discipline and structured body of knowledge should be undertaken cooperatively by the universities, government, and industry.

DISCUSSION

JACOB RABINOW: You described the innovative process in the civilian economy. A different set of rules applies in the space-defense sector, and we should understand that. The criteria for costs, performance, safety, and so on, are different.

Risk-taking

As to the personal characteristics of innovators, one of the things they deal with all the time is just plain luck. Therefore, successful innovators are inveterate risk-takers. Gambling is one of the most important things that an innovator does. He has to be willing to risk his money, his reputation, and his career; he shoots craps with everything he's got.

MYRON COLER: As we have noted, innovation is a process aimed at getting new ideas into society. This requires very creative and determined people and we should understand what kind of an environment they work in.

Creative people are, by and large, regarded as creative nuisances, not only because of their ideas, but often because they are intolerant of other people's ideas—especially other creative people's ideas. Some years ago one of the major colleges decided that it would accept almost nobody who wasn't a vice-president or president of his class in high school. I understand they were never so happy as when that class finally graduated.

DISCUSSION

We have heard of the importance of a champion in the innovative process. He is very important, for most creative individuals have needed, at one time or another, someone to push them into the ring, saying, reassuringly, "I don't think you'll get killed if you go in; I'm betting on you."

An Abstract Art

EMANUEL PIORE: One of the reasons we are having this conference is a conviction on the part of those who planned it that we need innovators and entrepreneurs in our society. To fill this need the engineering schools must assume a great responsibility of leadership. Since the war, engineering education has been in the direction of what Bill Shockley has called the mastery of specific fields of subject matter.

Some schools of engineering have become pretty much like an abstract art. What I mean is you can get just so much out of information theory, entropy, physical mechanics, and other technical fields; and then it is necessary to get into the pivotal aspects of engineering which have to do with the whole problem of entrepreneurship in our society.

J. HERBERT HOLLOMON: I would like to draw an analogy. Engineering schools, it seems to me, have become like most graduate English departments in America. With one or two exceptions, there isn't an English department that I know of that ever produced a creative writer. What seems to be happening in engineering education, on the majority of the campuses of this country, is equivalent to what has occurred in the English departments, where the student learns grammar, history, technique, semantics, etymology, and so on. Unfortunately, he does not become a creative writer.

ROBERT F. DALY: The English departments are short on the production of creative writers, but they do turn out legions of accomplished critics.

J. HERBERT HOLLOMON: A couple of years ago I undertook an analysis of many hundreds of abstracts of the final theses of Ph.D. candidates in engineering. Over 90 per cent of these theses involved an analytical, science-oriented dissertation associated with some particular field, such as electric field theory, aerodynamics, or network analysis. Less than 10 per cent of the theses were concerned with creative engineering design.

JOHN STEPHENS: Could you give an example of a subject in creative design which would be more appropriate for an engineering Ph.D. candidate than the science-oriented subjects they predominantly chose?

J. HERBERT HOLLOMON: The conceptual design of a new transportation system, for example. Let me add that creative design courses are included in the curricula of only a handful of the nation's engineering schools.

The Pendulum Swings

EMANUEL PIORE: I want to balance what I said a moment ago. We have to be careful that we don't paint a simple black and white picture of what is good and bad in engineering education. I can think of a few important inventions that have come from physicists and other "pure" scientists, who went into industry and fought innovative battles, but who had never been exposed to the kind of creative engineering education we have been talking about. We do not want to swing the pendulum so far the other way that we end up with a monolithic approach as to how you build great men who innovate.

DISCUSSION

Moreover, I think we would all agree that we do not want to leave the impression in our discussion that research is being degraded as an activity and that it has nothing to do with creativity. Good research is a highly creative enterprise, whether it's done in the engineering schools or in the science schools. Good research—and there's also very bad research, and we're not talking about that—requires a great deal of creativity.

EDGAR PIRET: About ten years ago our engineering schools were beginning to move more and more in the direction of the sciences. People said that our supply of basic knowledge was becoming depleted, and they also said we could no longer depend upon Europe as a source of that knowledge. These were at least some of the arguments that were made.

If you look at laboratories today in Europe, you will find that many which formerly were performing basic research are now turning more and more toward the *application* of science. They are trying to make use of information in the basic sciences which comes primarily now from the United States.

It is also interesting to note that the national research programs of some of the European countries—France, in particular—are increasingly being directed toward potential applications in industry.

The Master–Student Relationship

COSTAS ANAGNOSTOPOULOS: The state of teaching of innovation and creativity today is comparable to the state of the teaching of the natural sciences and other subjects in the Golden Age of Greece, when Pericles, Plato, Socrates and others taught by means of a master–student relationship. The subjects of innovation and creativity have not yet come to the stage where they can be "taught" as disciplines. So if my comparison is valid, we ought to have master–student relationships as a major tool for teaching invention, innovation and creativity, in general.

People, Purpose, and Environment

JACOB RABINOW: How do innovators emerge in large, multi-division companies? How are they trained and encouraged?

WILLIAM SHOCKLEY: Recalling my personal experience in the organizational framework of Bell Laboratories and the events that led to the development of the transistor, I have trouble seeing how one could consciously have improved upon the interrelationships that existed.

First of all, I accepted a job to go to Bell Laboratories as a physicist and work with C. A. Davidson. I had been a physics major and Mr. Davidson was one of the most distinguished American industrial physicists. When I got there they said, "We think you should get some perspective and work under Dr. Lewellyn on 'negative resistance' problems." So I worked with Dr. Lewellyn and put filters and things on lathes, things I knew nothing about. Next, they got me into the vacuum tube department and I worked with John Pierce and some other stimulating people. Then I decided I would prefer to work with Foster Nix, who had been asked to write an article on order and disorder in metal alloys. I felt that this was more in keeping with my academic training.

They let me make this shift, but then they got me into copper oxide rectifiers, something that was going on next door. I remembered that when I had been in the vacuum department, Mervin Kelly was making an effort to get me to put my permanent allegiance there. He had given me a big pep talk on how he foresaw the development of telephone exchanges that had no contacts. They would be run with vacuum tubes, he said. So from that time on I thought, "Sounds like a fine idea, but why do it with vacuum tubes? Why not do it with solids?" So I got involved primarily with amplifiers and tied them in with copper oxide devices. What had happened was this: I had been challenged by needs I had perceived all around me.

RICHARD MORSE: Basically, it was the environment that stimulated you.

WILLIAM SHOCKLEY: It was an area of need. You see, the needs impinged on us. It was a unique mixture of pressure, freedom, and exposure to needs. And it is hard for me to see how they could have gotten any more out of the situation by any other device.

J. HERBERT HOLLOMON: What that says is that creative engineering education requires putting some of the needs back into the universities.

JACK MORTON: Many people have said it in different ways, but I think what Bill Shockley said can be put in three words: People, purpose, and the environment, which is really two things, people and purpose together. There is no question about the value of getting the very best people you can get into the right positions, people who have creativity and mastery of a knowledge base.

I want to add that you can have all the good ideas, mastery of knowledge, and creative people, but until all of this is tied to a real purpose, the combination is sterile. They have to go together; there has to be a synapse among them.

C. STARK DRAPER: It seems to me that the essential ingredient is the right mental attitude coupled with the right environment. To just have the urge is not sufficient, because many people get the urge, but there has to be an ability to do something about it.

J. W. MASON: We have agreed that certain ingredients are needed for innovation in industry—the right environment, purpose, and timing. Now what can we as *educators* do? Well, we cannot do very much about the environment in industry. But we can do more about the individuals we put into that environment. We can do more about increasing the probability that the right person will be there at the right time. It seems to me that that is the function that we educators have to be concerned about.

DANIEL DE SIMONE: It seems an understatement of the power of education to say that educators can't do much about the environment in industry. The environment in industry is people; and all of the anti-innovative forces that we've been talking about are, one way or another, embodied in individuals whose attitudes toward innovation were largely shaped during the formative and impressionable years they spent in the educational system.

MYRON COLER: The educational system indeed has an enormous influence over the environment for creativity in industry, in government—and in the educational system itself. So we do well to begin in the schools, when we seek to stimulate innovation in the American economy.

CHAPTER 14

IMPROVING THE ENVIRONMENT FOR CREATIVITY

CALVIN W. TAYLOR*

CREATIVITY shows itself as a joint product of a person and his environment. When an engineer creates a new design, he does so within an environment of ideas and existing knowledge, of social needs, and of cultural attitudes concerning innovation. The attitudes may take many forms, and they may serve either to hinder or to assist the creative act.

The environmental factor is a dynamic one. It is exerted on the person not only here and now, at the time he is seeking to create, but also throughout most of his preceding life. The environmental forces that may affect his innovative behavior include the attitudes of his parents toward even the first question he asked as a child, the responses of teachers to his performance in school, the interests of playmates, the rewards society has given for his past contributions, and demands put upon him by his employer. These and many other environmental forces combine to affect the creative act he now is undertaking.

Research on the subject of creativity is reported in extensive literature.† From this literature emerge three generalizations, well validated, that are especially relevant to this chapter.

1. The set of human capabilities used to acquire, retain, and recall information is distinguishable from the set of capabilities used to solve a given problem or to devise a new design. The words

* Professor Taylor was chairman of a panel whose work provided the basis for this chapter. Other members of the panel were L. M. K. Boelter, Richard H. Bolt, Carl C. Chambers, Robert F. Daly, L. A. Hatch, Willis M. Hawkins, John A. Hrones, Edgar L. Piret, James B. Reswick, Herbert A. Shepard, Robert W. Schiessler.

† Summaries and interpretations of this research appear in the proceedings of the biennial national research conferences on *The Recognition and Development of Creative Talent,* University of Utah research conferences, 1955–1966.

retentivity and *creativity,* respectively, may be used to denote these two sets of capabilities.

2. Creativity involves exceedingly complex processes. It is a comfortable but misleading simplification to view them as processes occurring exclusively within an individual person. Instead, creative acts are the resultants of complex interactions among and within individuals, their environments, and the knowledge and experience available to them. An individual at any moment is himself the outcome of complex biological, social and experimental processes. Although some individuals appear to do better than others in combining and reorganizing information creatively, biological endowment in itself appears to be only a small part of the story.

3. The creative capabilities of individuals can be nourished, trained, and developed by providing appropriate environments and experiences. This generalization receives support from evidence that environments and experiences can be manipulated in such ways as to inhibit or cripple creative capabilities.

We are here concerned primarily with the environment associated with the professional education and training of scientists and engineers, from entrance into the freshman year of college through receipt of the academic degree at the bachelor's, master's, or doctor's level. Yet, this is a very small part of their educational lives. The parts of the environment only briefly considered here are those associated with pre-college schooling, post-college continuing education during the working years, and other aspects of life outside the processes of formal education. Although we will only briefly consider them, we should understand that influences on creativity before and after the professional educational experience may easily be more important than the formal education itself.

PRE-ENGINEERING SCHOOL PERIOD

The entire period prior to engineering school is a highly important formative one for students—perhaps the single most important one. The initial school years are where the educational environments have their first impacts and, though these can be potent, the child is still spending many more of his waking hours outside of school each calendar year than in school. As he grows older, he tends to have more teachers per year, more and more extracurricular activities, all of which increase both the number of educational factors affecting him and the percentage of his waking hours in which he is under the influence of school. Consequently, he has been programmed for approximately 18 years at home and in the world, including 12 or more years in school, before he starts his formal engineering education. Habits, patterns, and expectations have often crystalized quite firmly and have been stamped in through long years of practice.

Although this initial and lengthy background should not be overlooked, one should not feel that college freshmen are incapable of changing their patterns or becoming receptive to new ways of learning and thinking. Since attempts to encourage and cultivate creative processes and behaviors in students have to be started someplace, it may need to be initially in the engineering schools until more of the high schools and elementary schools deliberately devote some of their curriculum to fostering creative talent and creative experiences in students.

In any event, creativity has generally not been the most favored type of talent in schools. Engineering has the chance during at least parts of its curriculum to give the highest value to cultivating the creative potentials of its students. Instead of playing into their typical habit patterns, teachers can deliberately encourage students to display creative characteristics, such as sensing of problems, curiously inquiring, generating ideas of their own, tolerating uncertainties and ambiguities, and involving themselves deeply in work of their own.

The body of knowledge previously accumulated by students may be both an asset and a liability to them in terms of potential creative performances. Their knowledge may pattern them to think in certain orthodox ways and may tend to produce ruts of thinking from which it may be difficult for them to escape. In addition, they may have been exposed almost entirely to well-defined and documented knowledge, with little exposure to newer, more fuzzy knowledge or to the frontiers of knowledge or the unknowns that lie beyond the current boundaries. Engineering schools can capitalize on the opportunities of exposing them to young new areas, and to examples of rapidly expanding and changing knowledge, by giving some experiences at the fringes, and by opening up questions about unknowns as challenges for the future on which the oncoming generation can spend their talents, if they desire.

POST-ENGINEERING SCHOOL PERIOD

Engineers completing their university work should be impressed with the advantage of maintaining throughout their careers the intellectual qualities of the open mind toward new knowledge, which can be acquired through experience and further education. Using the mental tools and processes acquired during their technical education, they should seek and apply such later-acquired knowledge for the purpose of preparing the way for the acceptance and use of their technical ideas.

Education for engineers should be considered a lifetime process, beginning with the equivalent of medical internship and continuing with planned periods in the university environment. This implies that the universities prepare for such mature "refresher" students and creatively plan on how they might be used to impart experience to younger students.

ENGINEERING SCHOOL PERIOD

We have very briefly considered what comes before and after engineering school. Now we come to the engineering school period. Here teaching is the pivotal factor. When encouraging engineering students to generate and express ideas, a teacher may have to go against both his own well-established habits and theirs.

Our recommendations with respect to the engineering school period are based on several underlying premises:

1. Creativity, especially the self-generation of ideas, can be encouraged or discouraged in the engineering student by teachers and the teaching method.

2. In the process of communicating new information and new understanding, the teacher has many opportunities to request and catalyze both the generation and the synthesis of ideas by students, and many opportunities to inhibit the expression of ideas.

3. Interpersonal issues among students and faculty—their attitudes, perceptions, assumptions, and expectations about each other; the ways they ask questions; the ways they evaluate each other; and the ways they act toward each other—profoundly affect the environment for creative learning.

4. Idea expression by students is easily inhibited by teachers,

through attitudes and systems that discourage "hard" questions or that ridicule ideas.

5. Much knowledge has been developed to increase our understanding of creativity, what encourages *and* discourages it; the problem is how to bring this new understanding of creativity directly to bear in real teaching situations.

6. The creative process also occurs outside the classroom, when a student and teacher work together on a challenging problem or project—at any student level, freshman through postgraduate.

Nonengineering Consultants

Projects should be developed at certain engineering schools that are funded to support (a) educational innovations that will enhance creativity in students and (b) selected consultants who will spend enough time to share responsibility with the faculty in carrying out the educational innovations. The consultants should be nonengineering professors and each should be nationally recognized for his research on creativity. There should be a heavy commitment of the consultant's effort. It will not be enough for him just to come in and go out quickly without assuming responsibility. His direct participation in the classroom is necessary. He could, for example, serve as observer of creative teaching techniques and student response, and give almost immediate analyses of the results. He could suggest alternative approaches for the next day's class.

Fellow Students

Fellow students can be very important environmental factors. Classmates can be highly stimulating and provocative, at one extreme, or stifling and pressuring for control and conformity in other extreme instances. Some can be understanding and supportive and others, at times, can be unsympathetic and ostracizing. They can, through potentially powerful group pressures, attempt to "organize a person in", set their own climate and levels of excellence or mediocrity in scholarship, and establish their own pattern of expectations concerning levels or degrees of creative behavior to be allowed.

Engineering faculties should make a real effort to identify and nurture the creative sparks, the new-born ideas of the students, against potential negative effects from these fellow students. Maybe we need a course on how to nurture ideas for the first year of their lives, as we nurture new-born children. In addition, students should be used more often in teacher roles to show their fellow students what they have done creatively on their own. Students should also have experience in forming teams wherein one may emerge as the idea leader and the others as the cooperators in working on and implementing ideas.

Course Content

Course content is obviously a major challenge. The task in engineering is, among other things, to prepare a person to make value judgments and decisions a generation later in a society that may not resemble very much the society of his student days. Nevertheless, his college experience must bear a positive relationship to the demand of his immediate subsequent employment.

Curriculum boundaries should be flexible to eliminate superfluous requirements of knowledge and to accommodate new subjects. The problem always faced is how to make room for creative courses without swamping the present curriculum. One method is to maintain at a minimum the volume of knowledge the engineer must absorb and to facilitate his access to that knowledge. To this end, compendia of engineering knowledge and experience should be prepared. These compendia should probably be conceived along patterns considerably different from the present textbooks and references and make use of computer facilities.

Knowledge provides the stuff with which the creative minds work, so it is essential that the needed stuff is available in such minds. Materials to be learned should be cast into provocative styles, and students should be taught in such ways that they will *not* all end up by being merely "walking encyclopedias" or "walking libraries", but will be more efficient learners, users, and creative producers of knowledge.

It is strongly urged that vast efforts of an "educational engineering" nature be initiated to implement into educational programs all the pertinent basic research findings from the behavioral sciences. Capitalizing in this way may help provide time for creative activities. It might also enable students to finish their formal education at younger ages so that they would have completed all the "rituals required by the previous generation" to obtain their degrees. Obtaining this official stamp of approval early might enable them, if they desire, to feel more free and confident to spend perhaps all of the creative years during their twenties, as well as the rest of their career, in creative activities of their own.

Measurement of Student Performance

The grading systems customarily employed in engineering education are intended primarily to measure retentivity rather than creativity. In many cases, striving for good grades of this type inhibits the development of creativity. Experiments at changing the grading system usually end up with similar substitutes, although some institutions have eliminated or substantially depreciated formal grading in doctoral programs.

Engineering faculties should undertake a critical study of their grading systems with a view to developing more meaningful measures of student accomplishments, especially including accomplishments that reflect creative ability. A profile of sub-grades, including a sub-grade on creativity, may be of value; a combined over-all grade could be computed if desired.

In order to measure creative accomplishments, one must assign tasks that will give students opportunities to perform and produce creatively. One of the fascinating new educational challenges for teachers is the development of appropriate tasks, within the official curriculum, that elicit creative responses.

The approaches in industry to similar problems, as in salary determination, may contribute ideas on the grading problem. For example, special incentives could be provided to emphasize the importance of developing creative ability.

Another suggestion is to start a pilot program of one special creativity course (elective or required) in order to give students some experiences with their creative processes and potentials and to grade them on their capabilities and growth in creativity.

Extracurricular Activities

Any reasonably important design task involves a variety of technical disciplines. Programs or opportunities should therefore be created for students outside classroom hours to permit students of different disciplines to work together and create joint projects. In this way they could experience positive exchange of talents and learning, and also experience the restraints that multiple inputs of existing knowledge can put on design concepts, forcing compromises and change.

The creation of "outside school hours" workshops which consider and promote multi-discipline design projects would expose students to the uninhibited consideration of the types of group design decisions with which they must inevitably be faced in the future. This activity could well be the genesis of programs involving design laboratories, and the programs thus started would have much stronger motivation than "assigned" tasks.

Students should also be encouraged to generate their own ideas and programs for extracurricular activities. An official recognition and credit should somehow be given for these extracurricular activities and projects.

Administration

The role of an academic institution is to provide an environment in which all who live there learn to use their talents in the most effective manner. The professional school as well as the college of liberal arts has this objective. In addition, the professional school has the obligation of preparing its students for positions of imaginative leadership in specific areas of activity.

Administrators can greatly influence the environment. Among the many tools they have to work with are, of course, themselves and their behavior. Among the most important is the budgetary tool. If a single feature of an entire system is inflexible, the whole system is inflexible. The area that is often inflexible is the budgetary, the financial part. In tight budget years, little money is left on a discretionary basis.

There should be flexibility in budgetary matters, so that a substantial percentage of the annual budget can be allocated for discretionary use by appropriate administrators for the support of good ideas. This money should be currently available and not have been precommitted one, two or three years before.

The second tool the administrator can work with is recruitment of new faculty. He should avoid automatically staffing to maintain traditional ways of thinking. He should select some faculty members who are actively engaged in leading important engineering projects, not basic research.

The third tool concerns the promotion of existing faculty. The administrator should give due weight to innovative contributions to imaginative learning, as well as to the engineering profession. What he has done may be more important than what he has written.

Organizational change is the fourth tool. The structure of a university tends to become very rigid, with seniority rather than the ability to contribute new ideas determining the centers of power. Where necessary, the organizational structure should be changed to allow important new ideas to be tried and evaluated. A number of possibilities exist and new possibilities could be conceived: the creation of ad hoc organizations, competitive departments, new programs, new laboratories; permitting only limited periods of tenure in key administrative posts.

Two additional tools concern the behavior of the administrator. The first is a willingness to listen with enthusiasm to new ideas at all levels of authority, including the highest administrative posts. The second is that an administrator should be not only a receiver or catalyst or climate-provider for new ideas, but should also try to contribute his share of new ideas.

We all recognize, of course, that the administrator already has about all he can handle in controlling his operations, so that it will require great ability for him also to encourage innovation.

Pilot Ventures

A variety of pilot ventures should be established in several schools to try new techniques in fostering creativity. Simply prefacing a course title with "creative" does not constitute a creative engineering program. Illustrations of the variety of approaches are:

1. Developing creative thinking characteristics.
2. Developing creative personality and motivational characteristics.
3. Overcoming emotional hindrances and blocks to the creative processes.
4. Sensing the unknowns and launching creative ventures therein.
5. Drawing upon cybernetics and information theory, including attempts to increase the creativeness of the input (receptional) processes and the output (expressional) processes.
6. Developing special instructional media for creativity.
7. Modifying existing testing materials to make them suitable for situational training and other classroom instructional uses (such as have recently been developed for the Peace Corps).
8. Experimenting with related educational techniques, such as

inquiry training; discovery methods used in the arts and mathematics; programs in art, education, dance, and writing for fostering creativity; and various training programs in industry designed to develop creativity.
9. Utilizing the considerable recent research on creativity.
10. Encouraging the expansion of creativity workshops for teachers, such as those that have been held at Case, MIT, Dartmouth, Utah, Carnegie, Berkeley, UCLA, and the Commission on Engineering Education.
11. Building adequate communication among various action programs in the area of creativity in engineering education.
12. Developing engineering instructional materials for creativity programs. *This opens an almost entirely new field of educational challenge, since few of the existing materials have been designed with creativity in mind.*
13. Establishing an inter-university exchange of teachers who have been involved in creative engineering teaching.

These approaches, coupled with the other suggestions that have been made, could make a major contribution toward improving the environment for creativity in our institutions of higher education.

CONCLUDING DISCUSSION

The Influence of Fellow Students

B. RICHARD TEARE : I am not sure I fully understood what was meant about fellow students creating an environment.

CALVIN TAYLOR : Let me give you an illustration. I once visited one of the National Science Foundation's summer science programs for high-school students; they were a most exciting group. I stayed with them a day or two. Throughout this time—all through the evenings, too—they were talking about ideas and intellectual things. It wasn't all on science, either. During one of the breaks a girl said, "This is so different from the way it is back in my high school. Here, everyone wants to talk past hours about intellectual things. Back in school, when we are let out, the students get together, and often one of them, the union leader you might call him, will say, 'Well, we've got that assignment to do for tomorrow. If any of you does it, we will all be in trouble.' " I think that comment illustrates the impact of students on the behaviour of their fellows.

WILLIAM SHOCKLEY : I once tried some new approaches to science teaching with a class of ninth-grade students and teachers. It was obvious that some of the students were considerably quicker in catching on than the teachers were and were twiddling their thumbs while we tried bringing the others along. It seemed to me one might match impedances better if one could get these quicker students into a *teaching* role. We experimented with this. Ten of the students were given a two-week course and then asked to act as teachers for twenty additional students. I walked into a session where these ten students were teaching the second twenty and it was obvious at a glance that there were very strong interactions there. There was animation and attention. It occurs to me that in engineering education this sort of activity would satisfy another purpose. That is, there are always going to be some people who lead in the creation of ideas and others who use them and build upon them. Inter-student activities of the sort I've described might help students to see this and help to prepare them for later cooperative relationships.

JACK MORTON : The situation that Bill Shockley just described, in which some of the natural leaders take over the job in the class, is one which they will undoubtedly find when they start practicing either in government or industry. It very definitely happens.

The Number of Eggs Sold Last Year

JACOB RABINOW : You suggested making computers substantial memory stores for engineering students. I have a basic problem with that proposal. An inventor has to be able to retrieve information when he needs it, and if he doesn't have an acquaintance with it, how would he know what to get from a computer? He doesn't know what is essential, *a priori*. That is the problem. You don't get creativity if it's looking up the statistics of eggs sold last year in Ohio. That you can do with a computer, but it's different if you want to vary a problem and you don't know exactly how to solve it. Computers are no substitute for the creative aspect of the human brain.

Classroom Consultants on Creativity

S. M. MARCO : I would like to know more about the function of the "creativity" consultant mentioned by Professor Taylor. Would he, in effect, bring the research findings of experts in the field of creativity into the classroom?

CALVIN TAYLOR : The consultant would work with the teacher in a regular classroom setting. During the class hour, the consultant would perform the role of an observer, noting the teacher's behavior, the response of the students, and other factors. Afterward, he and the teacher would get together to talk about what had been observed and to point to relevant research findings in the field of creativity. He might suggest that perhaps the teacher would like to experiment with the new teaching techniques stemming from these research findings. If the teacher agrees, then the consultant would help the teacher to make the changes and observe what happens when they are tried. The consultant would thus be observer, evaluator, recommender, live consultant, and so on. He would not be just lecturing to groups of teachers. Rather, he would be right in there, working day by day, blow by blow, so to speak. The teacher would be in command; his advisor would be the consultant.

The Inelasticity of Time

JOSEPH LISTON: Where is the time going to come from to bring creative courses into engineering education? More than any other question, this one worries the educators. They have a four-year curriculum. They are hounded and importuned to put new science courses into the curriculum. What has happened is that a lot of the elements which were once in the curriculum have been eliminated. Therefore, to accommodate creative courses we either have to continue this process of elimination or allot more time.

CALVIN TAYLOR: I would hope that what engineering students are now learning about traditional subjects could be put across to them in less time, so that some time could be freed for the kinds of activities we have been talking about. It has been said that if we would put to use all that we now know about increasing the efficiency of teaching and learning we could give Ph.D.s in half the time we do now.

Curriculum "Cost–Benefit" Analyses

C. STARK DRAPER: At the Massachusetts Institute of Technology, in the Department of Aeronautics and Astronautics, we have been faced with this problem for some twenty years. We have had to add to the curriculum to give top students a vast amount of new technology and have had to bring into the aeronautical courses all the things that have recently come up in connection with space and astronautics.

The only solution I see in these kinds of situations is to go back and redo the whole structure of all the courses. It is not just a question of adding another course. You have to go back and search through the whole curriculum. And when you do, you find that the historical build-up of materials in these courses benefits quite a lot from the process of being subjected to critical analysis. I very definitely believe that as a result of this process we now give our students a better education, in less time, over a wider range. We effectively threw out substantially all the old laboratories because they were wasteful of time and because they usually do exactly what you don't want to do to creative students. They were mostly recipe-type experiments depending on the equipment. If you went to MIT, you may remember that you could go over to a little store and, for three cents apiece, you could buy a cover sheet that had blank spaces for all the observations you were to make. We simply threw those laboratory courses out completely and put in what are called project laboratories where the student can pick a project he wants to do from a wide variety of choices.

Moreover, computer consoles are tied in with these project labs. Each student can use this computer facility; he is trained to do that. And the computer frees a large amount of the student's time and the teacher's, too.

So it seems to me there is no hope in just adding courses and hoping for the best. You have to go back with a critical eye on every element and revamp the whole complex of education, including putting in things which will develop the imagination and resourcefulness of the students. It can be done and I can also assure you, having been the fellow who absorbed the brunt of the complaints that accompanied the changes, that it is not a pleasant or easy process.

JACOB RABINOW : Is it possible that your new techniques work at MIT because you have, on the average, a better set of students? It is obvious, for example, that if a school were to select only geniuses for students, it could condense a six-year course into three years.

Variations on a Medieval Theme

C. STARK DRAPER : The techniques do not require a special breed of students—just students who are properly motivated. The essential thing for motivation is a conducive environment. You need an environment where students are eagerly doing new things—an environment for creativity, instead of one that prompts a student to say, "Don't anybody do the problem for tomorrow because you could get us all into trouble." Finally, you need teachers who have a creative mental attitude. That helps enormously. But neither the students nor the teachers need to be supermen. All you need is to lay out a plan which is, shall we say, somewhat at variance with those of the old medieval universities.

WILLIAM BOLLAY : In view of our modern technology, a professional engineer requires five or six years of education to achieve an adequate degree of sophistication. It is practically impossible to crowd into a four-year curriculum sufficient basic sciences, the engineering sciences, and the kind of creative engineering experience that we are talking about.

CALVIN TAYLOR : We should not easily buy the word impossible, because it is a wide-open problem. If we brought to bear all of our capabilities and potential know-how, it might be much more possible than we realize. Instead of "crowding", as Professor Bollay suggests, these things could be done concurrently.

C. STARK DRAPER : At MIT the basic course has always been four years. To give you some rough figures, if you take one hundred freshmen, one-third will be graduate school material and we encourage them to go on to graduate school. Another third will have a terrible time in graduate school. It will be a waste of both their time and the instructor's. The remaining third can go either way.

Hitting the Target

But I want to tell you about the internship experience we provide at our Instrumentation Laboratory, where a couple of thousand people are working on a real budget. There, we did the Polaris guidance system and the Titan guidance, and we have also done the guidance system for the Apollo shot to the moon. These internes live in an atmosphere that has to be creative because they are not doing something under a grant from the National Science Foundation. They are competing with the world and they have to be creative, because if they don't drop the missile or the capsule on the target, you don't give them any kind of grade at all.

Changing the World

JACOB RABINOW : Should the universities turn out students to *fit* the world? With all due respect to my academic friends, I say the answer is, No. Their job is to *change* the world by encouraging their students to become world-changers. It is a tragedy just to try to fit them to the world, because the world is not right the way it is.

I once made a study as to whether you can predict what way a society will go politically in the future. Will it go fascist, communist, liberal, conservative? It turns out that one of the best ways of predicting world trends is to take a poll of the students in the colleges to see generally what their current views are. This is almost certain to tell you what a society will be like 20 years thereafter.

I did this a long time ago in an analysis of German students and found that, generally, the students were fascist. And the country went fascist. In Russia, when I was a child and the Czar was top man, the word "student" was synonymous with "left winger". You know what happened thereafter.

Toward the end of the 1940's, I asked a sampling of American students what they wanted out of life, and they said they didn't care about anything except getting good jobs and good positions. I decided then that the country would remain essentially conservative.

I don't know what the students want these days. But I feel strongly that it is the duty of an engineering school, not only to worry about whether students will be big bread winners, but also to influence them so that they, in turn, will influence society and make this world of ours a better place to live. That will take creativity—on the part of both the students *and* the engineering schools.

The Will to Think

WILLIAM SHOCKLEY : As we conclude our inquiry, I am reminded of something Enrico Fermi once said, which has not often been quoted. This was in the very early days of the atomic energy program. James Fisk and I at Bell Laboratories had been asked by the National Academy of Sciences to look into the possibility of using nuclear fission and its by-products.

We went to see Fermi to get some information on the nuclear process. This was before the Manhattan project, but somehow resources had been made available to Fermi and his colleagues so that they could do some experiments on nuclear fission. And he said to us, "We are bearing down much harder on this now, because we are being sustained; we have support. You see, since we are sure the experiments will go on, it gives us the *'will to think'*." This almost unknown phrase of Fermi's captures one of the essential ingredients of the innovative process, whether it be in industry, in government, or in engineering education. We must recognize and encourage those things which give us the "will to think", and thinking is much tougher than working or talking.

APPENDIX

PRINCIPAL CONTRIBUTORS

ROBERT B. BANKS is a Program Adviser for the Ford Foundation in Mexico, and former Dean of Engineering at the University of Illinois, Chicago.

WILLIAM BOLLAY is Visiting Professor of Aeronautics and Astronautics at Stanford University.

RAY E. BOLZ is Leonard Case Professor and Head of the Engineering Division of the Case Institute of Technology.

ROBERT C. DEAN, JR., is Professor of Engineering at Dartmouth College.

DANIEL V. DE SIMONE is Director of the Office of Invention and Innovation in the National Bureau of Standards.

CHARLES STARK DRAPER is Institute Professor and Director of the Instrumentation Laboratory at the Massachusetts Institute of Technology.

J. HERBERT HOLLOMON is the Assistant Secretary for Science and Technology, U.S. Department of Commerce.

RICHARD S. MORSE is a Senior Lecturer at the Alfred P. Sloan School of Management, Massachusetts Institute of Technology.

EMANUEL R. PIORE, who presided over the Woods Hole Conference, is Vice-President and Chief Scientist of the IBM Corporation.

JACOB RABINOW is President of the Rabinow Engineering Division, Control Data Corporation.

JOHN C. STEDMAN is Professor of Law at the University of Wisconsin School of Law.

CALVIN W. TAYLOR is Professor of Psychology at the University of Utah.

B. RICHARD TEARE is Institute Professor of Engineering at the Carnegie Institute of Technology.

APPENDIX

MEMBERS OF WOODS HOLE CONFERENCE

Costas E. Anagnostopoulos
  Monsanto Chemical Company
Robert B. Banks
  Ford Foundation
Donald W. Banner
  Borg-Warner Corporation
Fred J. Benson
  Texas A & M University
Donald L. Bitzer
  University of Illinois—Urbana
L. M. K. Boelter
  University of California—
  Los Angeles
William Bollay
  Stanford University
Richard H. Bolt
  Bolt, Beranek & Newman, Inc.
Ray E. Bolz
  Case Institute of Technology
Carl W. Borgmann
  Ford Foundation
David R. Boylan
  Iowa State University
Hugh Bradner
  University of California—La Jolla
Carl C. Chambers
  University of Pennsylvania
Robert A. Charpie
  Union Carbide Corporation
Robert G. Chollar
  The National Cash Register
  Company
Myron A. Coler
  New York University
Robert F. Daly
  Stanford Research Institute
Jack C. Davis (Capt. U.S.N.)
  Department of the Navy
Robert C. Dean, Jr.
  Dartmouth College
Daniel V. De Simone
  National Bureau of Standards
John H. Dessauer
  Xerox Corporation
Charles S. Draper
  Massachusetts Institute of
  Technology
Michael P. Gaus
  National Science Foundation
Robert J. Gillespie
  Sylvania Electric Products, Inc.
Peter C. Goldmark
  CBS Laboratories
Newman A. Hall
  Commission on Engineering
  Education
Seymour B. Hammond
  University of Utah
Charles Hasert
  U.S. Air Force
Lloyd A. Hatch
  Minnesota Mining & Manufacturing
Willis M. Hawkins
  Assistant Secretary of the Army
  for Research and Development
George Herbert
  Research Triangle Institute
Ivan R. Hershner, Jr.
  Department of the Army
James Hillier
  RCA Laboratories
Carroll A. Hockwalt
  St. Louis Research Council
J. Herbert Hollomon
  Assistant Secretary of Commerce
  for Science and Technology
James R. Hooper, Jr.
  Case Institute of Technology
Emanuel Horowitz
  National Bureau of Standards
John A. Hrones
  Case Institute of Technology
John M. Ide
  National Science Foundation
Harry S. Kantor
  U.S. Department of Labor
William C. Kelly
  National Academy of Sciences
Fred Kremer, Jr.
  AMC Corporation
Richard T. Kropf
  Belding Heminway Co., Inc.
Vincent H. Larson
  Northwestern University
Robert H. Linnell
  National Science Foundation
Joseph Liston
  Purdue University
George D. Lobingier
  Westinghouse Electric Corporation
Gordon J. MacDonald
  Institute for Defence Analyses

171

APPENDIX

S. M. MARCO
  The Ohio State University
J. W. MASON
  Georgia Institute of Technology
JAMES L. MASSEY
  University of Notre Dame
WILLIAM B. MCLEAN
  U.S. Naval Ordnance Test Station
HOWARD O. MCMAHON
  Arthur D. Little, Inc.
DAVID C. MILLER
  American Machine & Foundry Company
JAMES MITCHELL
  Woods Hole Oceanographic Institution
RICHARD S. MORSE
  Massachusetts Institute of Technology
JACK A. MORTON
  Bell Telephone Laboratories, Inc.
RALPH G. NEVINS
  Kansas State University
MORRIS B. PARLOFF
  National Institutes of Health
RICHARD E. PAULSON
  National Science Foundation
EMANUEL R. PIORE, *Presiding*
  IBM Corporation
EDGAR L. PIRET
  U.S. Scientific Attaché, Paris, France
GEORGE M. PRINCE
  Synectics, Inc.
STEPHEN QUIGLEY
  American Chemical Society
JACOB RABINOW
  Control Data Corporation
JAMES B. RESWICK
  Case Institute of Technology
LEON ROBBIN
  P. R. Mallory & Co., Inc.

SAMUEL RUBEN
  Ruben Laboratories
ROBERT W. SCHIESSLER
  Socony Mobil Oil Company
DONALD A. SCHON
  Harvard University
ANDREW S. SCHULTZ, JR.
  Cornell University
HERBERT A. SHEPARD
  Case Institute of Technology
WILLIAM SHOCKLEY
  Stanford University
JOHN C. STEDMAN
  University of Wisconsin
LOWELL W. STEELE
  General Electric Company
JOHN A. STEPHENS
  Excel-Mineral Company
CALVIN W. TAYLOR
  University of Utah
B. RICHARD TEARE
  Carnegie Institute of Technology
C. D. W. THORNTON
  International Telephone and Telegraph Corporation
RALPH TRESE
  University of Detroit
HOWARD TURNER
  Turner Construction Company
HAROLD VAGTBORG
  Southwest Research Center
CARL H. VESPER
  Stanford University
BROOKS WALKER
  Shasta Forrest Company
RICHARD R. WALTON
  Professional Inventor
ISRAEL WARSHAW
  National Science Foundation

INDEX

Abelson, Philip A.   viii
Accreditation, criteria   137
Act of Creation, The   43
Administrators, environment   161
Aerojet General Company   69
Africa, international responsibilities   27
Agriculture, its future   24
Air Force   83
Air pollution   28
   campus activity   132
   problems   119
Alumni pressures   137
American Medical Association, "world-of-work"   58
American Society for Engineering Education   15, 18
   inter-collegiate competitions   135
   literature for creative engineering   130
   market survey, employer–engineering needs   133
American Telephone and Telegraph Company, "world-of-work"   62
Ames Laboratory   69
Anagnostopoulos, Costas   145, 152
Anti-trust, influence on innovation   14, 16
Apollo shot   168
Application of theory   70
Appraisals
   market and projects   98
   techniques   149
Approaches to education   35–37
Arnold, John   49
Arrowsmith, William   12
Asia, international responsibilities   27
Associations, cooperation   18
Astronautics   166
Attitude   143
Automatic
   retrieval   82–84
   watch regulator   87–89
Awards
   Creative Engineering Teacher of the Year   18, 137
   innovators   72

Banks, Robert B.   136
Basic research, "people limited"   96
Bell Laboratories   76, 92, 152, 169
Biographies, creative engineers   130
Boelter, L. M.   73, 94
Bollay, William   41, 43, 166
Bolz, Ray E.   118
Boston
   entrepreneurs   102
   new enterprises   99
Business and creativity
   caution   41
   corporate decision makers   41
   live-and-let-live policy   42
   opposition to innovation   42
   procrastination   41
Business cases   150
Business versus creativity   38–40

California Institute of Technology   63
   Jet Propulsion Laboratory   69
Cambridge University   69
Campus activity   132
   commercial ventures   133
Capital, venture capital   97
Carnegie University   163
Case histories and problems   65–68, 130
Case Institute of Technology   163
Case problems, teaching methods   141
Case studies   129, 130
Charpie, Robert A.   73, 105
Chemical processes, investment   27
Chicago, new enterprises   98
Chrysler   66, 88
City College of New York   89
City planning   28
Classes
   new ideas   57
   size for creative education   140
Clemenceau, Georges   11
Clocks, regulators   87–89
"Clues to creative teaching"   59
Coler, Myron   150, 153

173

INDEX

Colleges
  cooperation 18
  creativity 139
  placement offices 135
  responsibility 126
  rewarding grades 141
Commercial ventures, campus activity 133
Commission on Engineering Education 15, 18, 111, 163
  literature on creative engineering 130
  market survey, employer–engineering needs 133
Communication
  ability 121
  necessity 43
  technology shaping society 8
Competition 131
  inter-collegiate 135
Computer, freedom for creativity 9
Concepts of engineering education 29–86
Conditions affecting creativity 3–18
Conservation, campus activity 132
Constraints 107–116
Consultants, environment 158
Contract of employer–employee, teaching 141
Cooperative
  education 69
  programs 100–102
  summer work 131
  ventures 150
Corporations
  entrepreneurship 95–106
  growth opportunities 100
  long-term planning 14
  management of innovation 14, 149
  support 149
Cost–time–market dynamics 149
Cost to resources 109
Course content 159, 160
Creative engineering education
  creativity versus retentive prowess 17
  factors 136, 137
  grading system 17
  improvement 17, 18
  orphaned by schools 12
  retentive prowess versus creativity 17
  school administration 136

society's needs 23–30
trade-off and constraints 107–116
Creative Engineering Teacher of the Year Award 18, 137
Creative process 74–94
  students, election and segregation 140
  teaching techniques 51
Creativity
  approaches to social problems 28
  attracting thinkers to engineering 59–61
  business versus creativity 38–40
  defining 3
  economic threats 40–42
  education 31–37
  engineering design, Ph.D. 7
  ethics and values 110
  evaluation of individual creativity 134
  excessive 61
  excluded from student's course 128
  factors influencing 49–62
  grading 160
  identity of individuals 139, 140
  "image" enhanced 134
  improving environment 154–169
  inquiring minds 52–56
  knowledge and creativity 56
  life history as factor 50–52
  opportunities 71–73
  psychological threats to 38–40
  self-regeneration 110
  social need 110
  sociological threats 40–42
  student education 107–114
  talent identified 134
  teacher education 107–114
  teacher encouragement 90
  teacher training, selected students 141
  teaching 139–146
  methods 157
  time for 8, 9
  workshops 63
Criteria, accreditation of engineering schools 137
Critical-mindedness 121
Cross-disciplines 43, 149, 160, 161
Cultural activities, non-work society 26
Cultures and engineering 38–45

INDEX

Curricula, creativeness 117
Cutler-Hammer 103

Daly, Robert F. 151
Dartmouth College 108, 110, 111, 112, 114, 163
Darwin, Charles R. 5
Data processing 27
Davidson, C. A. 152
Dean, Robert C., Jr. 93, 118, 146
de Balsac, Honoré 2
Defense
 government programs 30
 increasing investment 27
 technology transfers 96, 97
Department of Commerce vii, ix, 85
 "inventions wanted" 65
 national competitions 135
 Technical Advisory Board ix
Descartes, René 64
Design
 encouragement 132
 laboratories 16
 motor vehicles 28
De Simone, Daniel 146, 153
Development 31, 136
 faculty 123-127
 international responsibilities 27
 investment increasing 27
 thinking process 142
Diamond, Harry 92
Discipline
 discipline versus imagination 108, 111
 Gemini V, cross-disciplinary success 34
Draper, Charles Stark ix, 8, 9, 14, 106, 109, 110, 145, 153, 167, 168

Eckert and Mauchly Corporation 86
Eckert, J. Presper 86
Economic aspects of teaching 141
Economic balance of cost to return for innovation 41
Economic threats to creativity 40-42
Edison, Thomas 78
Education
 aims 118-121
 concepts 29-86
 conditions affecting creativity 3-18

cooperative student 69
creativity needs 36
engineering, implementation 159
intern 69
invention 139-146
objectives 117-122
role in engineering creativity 33-35
summarized 19
U.S. Office of Education 53, 62
use of wealth 26
Egypt, human values 6
Eiseley, Loren, *The Immense Journey* 5
Electronics, investment increasing 27
Energy 119
Engineering
 creativity and elements 31-33
 culture 38-45
 design, Ph.D. theses 69
 educational objectives 117-122
 human factors 120
 methods and use 119
Engineering education 23-30
 approach 35-37
 creative act removed 23
 encouraging student inventors 90
 experience 117
 improvement 118
 intern programs 69
 internship 15
 investment increasing 27
 needs of society 7, 8, 14
 neglect 7
 new directions 63-73
 objectives 1, 121
 post-education problems 38-45
 post-world war 2, 23
 predetermined methods, teaching fault 36
 science-based 23
 seminars 70, 71
 social problems, related 134
 source 30
 standards 121
 teacher experience 112
 teachers to be used 108
 teacher-student relationship 54
Engineering schools, criteria for accreditation 137
Enterprises, ingredients 98
Entrepreneur and entrepreneurship 15, 95-106, 149
 contributions 99
 educational 109, 111, 147-153

175

INDEX

Entrepreneur and entrepreneurship—*cont.*
  foreign students 111
  student workshops 113
Environment
  administrators 161
  budgetary problems 161
  corporate 149
  course content 159, 160
  creativity 139
  cross-disciplines 160
  engineering school period 157–163
  extracurricular activities 160, 161
  faculty recruitment 161
  fellow students 158, 159
  grading 160
  improving for creativity 154–169
  industrial 149
  new enterprise 98
  non-engineering consultants 158
  pilot ventures 162, 163
  post-engineering school 157
  pre-college 155
  pre-engineering school 155, 156
  realism 110
  "real-world" activity 131
Environmental pollution 5–7
Esso Educational Foundation 60
Ethics, teaching 141
Evaluations 120
Experimentation 137
Extracurricular activities 160, 161

Factors, creative engineering education 136–137
Faculty
  collateral assistance 125
  cross-disciplines 126
  development 123–127
  entrepreneurs 148
  environment 157
  exchange 135
  industrial experience 125, 136
  industrial part-time instructors 126
  innovators 148
  motivation 123–127
  publication 125
  recruitment 161
  rewards 124
  teacher exchange 163
  training programs 136
  travelling professorships 126

Fairchild, Sherman 92
Federal government
  case programs 15
  influences 14, 16
  research 14
Fellowships 15, 135
Fermi, Enrico 169
Financing innovative ideas 98
Fisk, James 169
Ford Foundation, residencies in engineering practice 136
"Forefront" engineering activity 132
Foreign aid programs, technical assistance 27
Foreign students, entrepreneurs 111
Foundations
  cooperation 18
  faculty assistance 127
  pressures 137
Free-time society 7
Freud, Sigmund 44

Gallagher, James 59
Gandhi, Mahatma 6
Gardner, John W. 6
Gas turbine 66
Gemini V 34
General Electric 104
Germany, pulse-jet 63
Gilbarg, David 83
Gillette Company 103
Golden Age 152
Göttingen, University of 69
Government
  climate 148
  cooperation 18
  development 149
  faculty assistance 127
  interest in engineering education 117
  policy 149
  pressures 137
  programs, limitations 30
  research 149
  summer projects 137
Grading 160
  hindrance to creativity 140
  rewarding creativity 141
Graduate schools, new enterprises 98
Graduate theses, concept 132
Gross National Product, contribution to technology 5

INDEX

Hammond, Dr. 60
Harmon, Lindsey 61
Hart, Senator Philip 10
Harvard Business School 138
Hatch, Lloyd 146
Heron 4
High schools
 creative teachers 140, 141
 creativity 139
 environment 156
Highway safety, campus activity 132
Hilch 70
Hollomon, J. Herbert ix, 7, 8, 44, 108, 151, 153
Hospitals, patients weighed in bed 112
Housing problems 119
Hudson 59
Hutchinson, W. L. 60
Hyman, R. 56, 57

Ideas
 expression, environment 157
 selling 14
Imagination versus discipline 108, 111
Immense Journey, The 5
India, Western technology and Gandhi 6
Industry
 campus commercial ventures 133
 case studies and experience 129
 climate 148
 cooperation 18
 experts, case study assistance 130
 faculty assistance 127
 faculty employment 125
 instructors in creativity 141
 internship 149
 part-time faculty 126
 teaching engineering 109
Inertia 75
Information
 gathering 120
 handling systems 119
Innovation
 appreciation of process 120
 consequences of change 4, 5
 cooperation 100–102
 education 147–153
 educational institutions 148
 elements 95–106
 entrepreneurship 95–106
 explained 4
 financing 98
 introducing 149
 labor opposition 42
 manipulators and change 5–7
 teaching 148
 technology transfers 96, 97
 venture capital 97
Instrumentation laboratory, Massachusetts Institute of Technology 69, 106
Inter-business relations 14
Inter-collegiate competitions 135
International Business Machines Corporation 103–105
International responsibilities
 political stability 27
 technical problems 27
Internship 15, 131, 149, 150
 programs, engineering education 69
Invention
 appraisal 14
 consequences of change 4, 5
 education for 139–146
 explained 4
 "morphological" approach 76
 nature of 75–77
 political and social feasibility 29
 process 74–94
 protection 14
 students 16
 teaching 139–146
 technology transfers 96, 97
Inventors
 recognition 15
 students, encouragement 90
 universities 73
 university projects 15

Jablonski, J. R. 54
Jefferson, Thomas 11
Jet Propulsion Laboratory, California Institute of Technology 69
Johnson–Rhabek clutch 85

Kelly, Mervin 152
Kettering, Charles 2, 12, 77
Knowledge and creativity 56–59
Koestler, *The Act of Creation* 43
Kremlin 44

INDEX

Labor and innovation 42
Laboratories
  design 16
  engineering schools, integration 132
Land, Edwin 13
Larrabee, Eric vii
Latin America, international responsibilities 27
Lectureships 135
Legal and proprietary rights and problems, teaching 141
Lewellyn, Dr. 152
Lincoln, Abraham 81
Liston, Joseph 145, 146, 166
Literature 130
Lockheed 69

Madison Avenue 44
Magnetic clutch 84
Malina, Frank 69
Marco, S. M. 165
Market
  analysis 14
  appraisal 98
  employer–engineering needs 133
Marketing 147
Marshall, Alfred 20
Mason, J. W. 153
Massachusetts Institute of Technology 49, 85, 106, 163, 166, 167, 168
  Department of Aeronautics 68
  Instrumentation Laboratory 69
Material handling problems 119
McLuhan, Marshall 2
Measurement, grades 160
Methods of teaching invention 65–68, 128–138
Moore, Mrs. Lesley ix
"Morphological" approach to invention 63, 76
Morse, Richard 153
Morton, Jack 92, 105, 144, 153, 165
Motion pictures, stereo 84
Motivation
  competition 131
  faculty 123–127
Motor vehicle design 28
  magnetic clutch 86
Multiple solutions 137
Mylar balloons 67

NASA 55, 69
National Academy of Engineering vii, ix
  market surveys, employer–engineering needs 133
National Academy of Sciences ix, 169
National Bureau of Standards 68, 76, 85
National competitions 135
National Institute of Health 93
National Inventors Council ix, 12, 41
  competitions 135
National Recovery Administration 89
National Science Foundation vii, ix, 62, 111, 168
Nature of invention 75–77
Navy Bureau of Aeronautics 63
Nix, Foster 152
Non-engineering consultants 158
"Non-work" society 7
  advent 25–27

Observation 143
Office of Education, U.S. 53, 62
Opportunities 115–169
Optimist's Club of Washington 84
Ortega y Gasset, José 11

Palo Alto, new enterprises 99
Parents, environment and creativity 154
Patents
  law, influence on innovation 14
  office 82, 84–86, 90
  protection 41
  teaching 141
Patients, weighed in bed 112
Peace Corps, devices needed 134
Pennsylvania State University 54
Pericles 152
Philadelphia, new enterprises 98
Philanthropies, pressures 137
Photography, blurred image 83
Pierce, John 152
Pilot ventures 162, 163
Piore, Emanuel R. viii, 62, 93, 151
Piret, Edgar L. 138, 152
Plato 152
Polaris 168
Pollution 28
Post-education problems 38–45

INDEX

Pre-college environment 155
Problems, solution 119–121
Processes, encouragement 132
Production
  costs 147
  encouragement 132
  gross national products 5
Professional associations 18
Professional education experience 155
Projects
  appraisal 98
  students' 130–131
Proprietary rights, teaching 141
Publication, faculty experience in creative engineering 125
Pulse-jet 63

Rabinow, Jacob 10, 102, 145, 146, 150, 152, 165–168
Rabinow Electronics 103
"Real-world" situations 137, 141, 142
Recreation, "non-work" society 26
Regulations, influence on innovation 14
Research 136
  entrepreneurship 148
  faculty 124
  federal funds 14
  innovation 148
  international responsibilities 27
  investment increasing 27
  new enterprises 98
Research and development, restrictions 100
Residencies, engineering practice 136
Resource conservation, campus activity 132
Rhabek, Johnson–Rhabek clutch 85

Salversan 78
Satellite
  Soviet Union 12
  "yo-yo" 70
Schon, Donald 104
Schools
  creative engineering education 136
  criteria for accreditation 137
Science
  engineering 108
  fairs, engineering competition 135

high school courses 140
technology interactions 136
Self-development 121
Self-discovery 137
Service industries 24, 25
Shepard, Herbert 146
Shockley, William 19, 62, 76, 77, 138, 151, 152, 164, 169
"606" approach 78
Snow, C. P. 45
Social problems, engineering education related 134
Sociological threats to creativity 41–42
Socrates 152
Soviet Union, satellite 12
Space 150, 166
  government program 30
  international responsibilities 27
  investment increasing 27
  Soviet Union 12
  technology transfers 96, 97
Speakers on creativity 141
Special courses 144
Stanford University 68, 69, 84, 130, 138
Stedman, John 9, 10
Stephens, John 151
Stereo motion pictures 84
Strategies
  market surveys 133
  teaching methods 128–138
Strong, Professor 64
Students
  environment 158, 159
  experience 150
  inventions 16
Suchman, Richard 53
Summer "real-world" work 131
Symposia 144
Synthesis, process of 137
Systems, encouragement 132

Taxes, influence on innovation 14, 16
Taylor, Calvin W. 18, 43, 45, 64, 93, 164–168
  "Clues to creative teaching" 59
Teacher-teaching
  advancement for creative education 140
  alterations in nature of teaching 109
  case studies 129, 130
  course concepts 124

179

INDEX

Teacher-teaching—*cont.*
  curriculum directions 124
  engineering experience 112
  exchange 163
  faculty research 124
  methods and materials 129, 130
  new methods 124
  programs 16
  projects for students 130, 131
  "real-world" activity 131
  role in engineering education 108
  schools or industry 109
  strategies and methods 128–138
  student relationship 54
  training in techniques of creativity 141
Teare, B. Richard 164
Technology 31
  competitive advancement 14
  enterprise 14
  investment 27, 28
  science interactions 138
  service industries, challenge 25
  transfers 96, 97
  understanding 16
  use of decreased work time 26
Theory, application 70
Theses, graduate schools 132
Thornton, C. D. W. 103
3M 104
Timepieces, regulators 87–89
Timing 147
Titan 168
Trade-off and constraints 107–116
Trade secrets
  protection 14, 41
  teaching 141
Traffic safety 28
Transportation problems 119
Travelling professorships 126

U.S. Department of Commerce *see* Department of Commerce
U.S. Navy Bureau of Aeronautics 66

U.S. Office of Education 53, 62
Universities *see* Colleges
University of California 163
University of Göttingen 69
"Upalator" 113
Urbanization, environment affected 24
Utah, "world-of-work" study 58

Venture capital 14, 97, 149
  new enterprises 89
Vesper, Carl 138
von Braun, Werner 60
von Karman, Theodore 69
von Ohain, Hans 69

Walker, Brooks 61, 144
Wallace, Alfred Russel 5
Washington, D.C. 44
Watches, regulators 87–89
Water pollution 28
  campus activity 132
  problems 119
Water supplies 28
Weighing hospital patients in bed 112
Westinghouse Corporation, engineering competitions 135
Wheelchairs 114
Whitehead, Alfred North 1
Whittle, Frank 69
Winslow 85
Woods Hole (Mass.) Conference vii, viii, ix, 7, 11, 13, 14
Woods Hole Oceanographic Institutions ix
Workshops 144
"World-of-work" performance 49–62

"Yo-yo", satellites 70

Zwicky, Fritz 63

T
62
E3
1968